The History of
Rome

Also available from
Speculative Grammarian Press

The Speculative Grammarian Essential Guide to Linguistics

THE
HISTORY
OF
ROME

FROM THE FOUNDING OF THE CITY
TO THE FALL OF THE EMPIRE

WRITTEN AND ILLUSTRATED BY

TIM PULJU

Occasional Lecturer in Classics
at Dartmouth College

Speculative Grammarian Press

Published by
Speculative Grammarian Press
www.specgram.com

This book was typeset by Tim Pulju using several different fonts, mostly Times New Roman, but also a bit of Garamond, Lucida Calligraphy, and Lucida Handwriting, plus mere smidges of Helvetica, Monotype Corsiva, Old English Text MT, and (on the spine and front cover) Century and Book Antiqua. Frankly, I can't see why anyone would care to know all that, but it seems to be customary to include font information on a book's publication page, so I went ahead and included it.

The cover illustration shows the Arch of Titus as it looked when last I saw it, back in 1998. I expect it looks about the same now as it did then.

Table of Contents

List of maps vii

Boring Prelude ix

Chapter One *in which our heroes build a city* 1

Dramatic Interlude 13

Chapter Two *in which the Romans spread their dominion* 15

Musical Interlude 25

Chapter Three *in which a surprisingly large amount of stuff happens* 27

Epistolary Interlude 33

Chapter Four *in which there are some stylistic oddities* 35

Psychiatric Interlude 49

Chapter Five *in which a republic becomes an empire* 51

Strange Interlude 61

Chapter Six *in which we meet emperors of various sorts* 63

Poetic Interlude 73

Chapter Seven *in which there are five good emperors* 75

Pugilistic Interlude 83

Chapter Eight *in which things fall apart* 85

Lexicographic Interlude 95

Chapter Nine *in which the Romans put Humpty together again* 97

Promotional Interlude 107

Chapter Ten *in which our story comes to an end* 109

Consolatory Postlude 125

Index of personal names 127

List of Maps

Italy and Environs, c. 500 BC 1

The Mediterranean World, c. 200 BC 15

A Roman View of the World, c. 115 BC 21

Map of the Roman World in 44 BC 35

The Roman Empire, 14 AD 51

The City of Rome in the late 1st century AD 63

The Roman Empire in the 2nd century AD 75

The Roman World in the late 260's AD 85

The Roman World in 324 AD 97

The Roman World in late 395 AD 109

The Post-Roman World in 500 AD 122

The City of Rome in the late 5th century AD 125

Boring Prelude

You can skip this part if you want.
Really, I won't mind. How could I mind? I won't even know.

I originally wrote this book for students in my first-year Latin courses at Dartmouth College. In those classes, we have to spend so much time cramming in grammar and vocabulary that there's little class time left over for learning Roman history. That's a shame, because Roman history is fun, plus learning Latin is more fun if you have some idea of, say, who Cicero was, or why Caesar was conquering Gaul anyway. So I decided to write up a short history of Rome for my students to read outside of class, if they wanted to, or to toss in the recycling bin, if they didn't want to read it. To try to encourage them to do the former rather than the latter, I tried to make it entertaining. Some of my students, possibly those who wanted to get good grades without doing a lot of work, claimed that they did find it entertaining. So maybe people who aren't my students will like it too.

One thing that most people don't find very entertaining is technical terminology in foreign languages. Therefore, this history leaves out lots of terms and associated concepts that you'll find in other, stodgier works, such as *iugerum, comitia centuriata*, and *magister peditum praesentalis*. If you want to learn those sorts of terms, you could get one of the many other Roman history books that are out there. Many of them are quite good, stodgy though they may be. I haven't included a list of such books, because if you're really interested in them, you're probably clever enough to find them on your own.

I should perhaps mention that, entertaining or not (hopefully the former), this book is historically reliable, except for things that are obviously meant as jokes. Thus, on p. 18, when I tell you that Rome declared war on Carthage in 149 BC, you can believe it. But when I tell you that the Romans sold tickets to people who wanted to watch the war, you might want to swallow a grain or two of salt.

One last thing that this book has to make it entertaining is pictures. Nowadays, all the other books have pictures too, but their pictures are actual photographs of works of art, or ruined cities in northern Africa, or so on. I thought it would be more fun to draw my own pictures, and also cheaper, since I wouldn't have to pay for the rights to use other people's photographs. It's true that I don't have any artistic training, so the pictures aren't, to use a technical term from the world of art criticism, particularly "good." However, I like to think that they have a naive charm, not unlike that of the text itself.

I also drew the maps. Like the pictures, they're kind of amateurish, but at least they tell you where to find cities, provinces, rivers, etc. Unlike some writers of history books, I'm well aware that not every American knows where the Danube River is, let alone Palmyra.

Anyway, now you know why I wrote this book the way I did. If you don't really care, maybe you should have skipped this prelude, as per my suggestion above, and gone straight to Chapter One. Too late now.

The Author Attempts to
Draw a Picture of Caesar

THE HISTORY OF ROME

Chapter One

in which our heroes build a city,
fight the neighbors,
and meet some elephants

Civilization
Matrix

	Yes	Somewhat	Not Very
Etruscans	✓		
Latins		✓	
Greeks	✓		
Sabines			✓

As you can see from this map, Italy is full of mountains. How Winston Churchill came to view it as "the soft underbelly of Europe" is not exactly clear.

Corsica (Future home of Napoleon Bonaparte)

Sardinia (no one famous ever came from here)

Spain ← thataway

Carthage

Africa (Elephants actually lived west of here, near the Atlas Mountains. This one is just visiting.)

Sicily (future home of Vito Corleone)

Greece → over here

Tarentum

Mt. Vesuvius

Mt. Etna

Italy and environs, c. 500 BC

Rome: The Beginnings

About 3000 years ago, there were no Romans, just a bunch of tribal people living in Italy, herding cattle, worshipping a paternal sky god, and doing other sorts of things that tribal people do. Probably drinking a lot of wine, because there are plenty of grapes in Italy, and herding cattle all day long can get pretty boring.

Some of these people lived near the center of the southwestern coast of Italy, mostly to the southeast of the Tiber River. They called themselves Latins, for no apparent reason, and they called their country Latium. The Latins had a few towns, like Alba Longa, which made them more civilized than some of their neighbors, such as the

An Estruscan Woman

Sabines who lived in the mountains of central Italy. However, elsewhere there were people who were much more cultured than the Latins. To the northwest of Latium, in Etruria, lived the Etruscans, elegant people who spoke a funny language and liked mirrors and cemeteries. To the southeast, there were even more cultured people who called themselves Hellenes. But the Latins weren't going to stand for that. Hellenes, in their opinion, was a stupid name, and they preferred to call the southeasterners Greeks. Most people today follow their example, except for the Greeks themselves, who insist on calling themselves Hellenes still, even though they don't pronounce the name properly anymore. Still, it's better than the Middle Ages, when the Greeks very confusingly called themselves Romans, even though by that time they didn't live anywhere near Rome.

Which gets us back to our main topic, Rome, which, I confess, I almost forgot about in the course of the last paragraph. Some of the Latins lived on some hills near an island in the Tiber, which was a convenient place for fording the river if you were headed southeast from Etruria, and also a good place for boats to go down the river and trade with Greeks or other people who came by sea to the river mouth. So some enterprising Latins set up a cattle market at the foot of the hills, as well as a more generalized open air market, called the Forum, in a swampy area between two of the main hills. But they kept living on the hills, because it was easier to defend the hills if some marauding neighboring tribesmen happened by. Besides, no one wants to live in a swamp or a cattle market.

Over the next couple of centuries, somehow or other, the settlement on the hills expanded and developed into a city, ruled by kings, which dominated the rest of the Latins, and was called Rome. Unfortunately, no one knows exactly how any of this happened, because no one at the time bothered to write any descriptions of what was going on, and now they're all long dead. Obviously,

The Etruscan Language

Chances are that you've heard some nonsense about the mysterious Etruscan language, still undeciphered despite the best efforts of generations of scholars, and probably proof that Etruscan civilization was founded by spacemen or something. Bah! Although Etruscan is, in fact, unrelated to other languages of Italy, there's still nothing particularly weird about it. It's written in an alphabet that's similar to other ancient alphabets of Italy, so scholars can pronounce Etruscan words easily enough. The problem is that most Etruscan texts are very short and boring. A lot of them are tomb inscriptions, saying things like "Tanaquil Trebia, wife of Arruns Vibenna, son of Arruns." There are some longer texts, but unfortunately, we don't know what most of the words mean, and there are no extant copies of the Etruscan dictionaries that Roman scholars put together.

someone was doing something—building temples, draining the swamp ("Hey," said some clever Roman, "I bet the Forum would be a lot more fun to shop at if there weren't so many mosquitoes")—and one of those somebodies eventually made himself the first king. But since no one knows who or when, modern historians spend most of their time arguing about things like how much the growth of early Rome was the result of Etruscan influence.

But we're not going to worry about the extent of Etruscan influence in this book, because that might require us to start talking about really boring topics like pottery. Instead, we're going to review a story about the early days of Rome which no one believes in nowadays, but which everyone knows anyway, because it's a good story, and it's the only one we've got. This story comes from an ancient Roman named Livy, who, writing many centuries after Rome was founded, tried to put together a coherent history based on what he could cobble together from various legends and traditional stories. He admitted that most of what he wrote probably wasn't historically accurate, but he said it was worth reading anyway. So let's read it.

The Early History of Rome, as told by Livy (somewhat modified, rearranged, and abridged)

Once upon a time in the year 753 BC, in the city of Alba Longa, two youths, twin brothers from the countryside, appeared at the king's house. They called themselves Romulus and Remus, and they explained that they were there to kill the king and put the king's brother (their grandfather) on the throne. And that's just what they did. Next, they went off to the hills near the Tiber and decided to found a city. Romulus wanted to found it in one place, Remus in another, so Romulus killed Remus and then went on with his nation-building enterprise. He populated his city (which, modestly, he named "Rome") with the dregs of society, many of them criminals who had fled from other towns, and then got wives for them by kidnapping a bunch of Sabine women. He also spent lots of time fighting little wars against neighboring communities. Eventually, Romulus mysteriously disappeared during a thunderstorm one day, at a time when he happened to be standing near a group of Roman nobles who didn't like him very much. The nobles claimed that he had flown up to heaven, turned into a god, and changed his name to Quirinus, which I guess is what you did in those days when you became a god. Strangely, the bulk of the population accepted the nobles' claim and started to worship Quirinus. One suspects that the bulk of the population was not all that bright.

The Romans, who needed a new king, eventually chose someone as unlike Romulus as they could, a peaceful, pious Sabine named Numa Pompilius. Numa did lots of religious stuff, then died and was succeeded by a king named Tullus Hostilius. As you can tell from Tullus' last name, the Romans were tired of being peaceful, so they picked a king who was bound to revive the tradition of attacking the neighbors. After Tullus, the next king was Numa's grandson Ancus Marcius, who was pretty boring, so we'll say no more about him.

Romulus Goes up to Heaven

When Ancus died, an Etruscan immigrant named Tarquinius Priscus, or Tarquin for short, got himself chosen king, to the exclusion of Ancus' young sons. Naturally, once they were older, the sons weren't too happy about this, so they killed Tarquin as part of plot to retake the throne. However, Tarquin's son-in-law Servius Tullius outwitted them and got the people to choose him instead.

Modern historians think there may really have been a Servius Tullius. The Romans themselves, many centuries later, credited Servius with reforming the organizational scheme of society, government, and the army. He was so impressive a king that the Romans thought he had built a wall around Rome which, according to archeologists, actually postdates him by a couple hundred years. However, not everyone was impressed, especially not one of Tarquin's sons, known as Tarquinius Superbus. This younger Tarquin was married to Servius' daughter, but that didn't help Servius out when Tarquin decided that he ought to be king instead. Yes, you guessed it, Tarquin killed Servius and made himself king.

Tarquin's Latin nickname, Superbus, doesn't mean "superb," it means "proud" or "arrogant" (it would be a good nickname for certain countries, such as France and Lesotho). The Romans didn't care for Tarquin much. He conquered a lot of neighboring peoples, using the army that Servius Tullius had reorganized, and he built some temples, but the people complained about having to fight in his wars and pay high taxes. Eventually, there was a revolution, and Tarquin was kicked out of the city.

Livy says that the revolution happened in the year 509 BC. There probably really was a revolution around that time, and it probably did involve throwing out a king whose family was of Etruscan origin. The leader of the revolt was a man named Lucius Junius Brutus, whose last name means "stupid" in Latin. But maybe Brutus wasn't so stupid after all: having noticed that Roman kings had a way of getting killed or overthrown, he declined to become king himself, but instead instituted a republic with two chief magistrates (known, eventually, as "consuls") who ruled jointly for a one-year period. Of course, he didn't go so far as to decline the honor of being one of the magistrates himself, in which position he had the pleasure of executing his own sons when they got caught plotting to put Tarquin back on the throne.

So much for the seven kings. And so much, also, for just repeating what Livy said because we can't think of anything better. From now on, although the story relies on Livy quite a bit, there are other sources of information which help us to have a more realistic picture of what was going on. And Livy himself becomes gradually more reliable the closer he gets to his own time. So what follows will be a story much less colorful than the legend of Romulus the fratricide, but hopefully a little more historically accurate. Not that you could get any random group of five modern scholars to agree on any of it. It's hard enough to get modern scholars to agree on where to go for dinner.

The Roman Republic: The First 250 Years

The Roman Republic had been founded by leading aristocratic families who called themselves patricians. It didn't take long for the non-patricians to notice that the patricians defined a republic as "a system of government in which the patricians have all the rights." The relatively poor non-patricians, who were called plebeians, were particularly upset about things like being sold into slavery when they couldn't pay their debts. Unfortunately, since the patricians had all the wealth and power, there didn't seem to be much the plebeians could do to change things.

However, it turned out that while the Romans had been distracted with their revolution, various neighboring communities whom the kings had subjugated had taken the opportunity to break free of Rome's yoke. Oops! Even worse, new peoples named Volsci and Aequi had settled in the neighborhood and were making trouble. So the patricians thought that Rome should continue to raise armies and go out to fight the neighbors.

The plebeians saw their chance. Next time the patricians called the plebeians together and said, "Okay, guys, get your weapons and let's go conquer the neighbors," the plebeians replied, "Sorry, we're going to go have a meeting on the Aventine Hill instead. No patricians allowed." And they refused to come back from the Aventine Hill until the patricians gave them some rights. Through the use of this and similar tactics, the plebeians won a variety of concessions over the next decades, including the right to put Twelve Tables in the middle of the Forum (originally, there were only Ten Tables, but everyone agreed that ten just wasn't enough) and the right to have their own magistrates called tribunes.

What with all the civil strife, it was hard for the Romans to war down their proud neighbors the way they wanted to, but the end of the 5th century BC, they had their act together again. The Volsci and Aequi were defeated, the other Latins acknowledged Rome's hegemony, and the Romans even conquered a nearby Etruscan city named Veii. So by the year 390 BC, the Romans were feeling their oats, flexing their muscles, strutting their stuff, and generally employing so many metaphors that it was plain they were riding for a fall.

The fall came in the form of a group of rampaging Gauls. Gauls were fair-skinned barbarians with flaxen hair and plaid trousers; one imagines that Gallic boys would have been very popular with ancient Greek intellectuals. The Gauls were not, however, all that popular in Italy, which they had started invading from the north around 600 BC. In the year 390, a Gallic army that was raiding central Italy took time off from fighting the Etruscans to attack Rome. They whupped a Roman army, captured the whole city except for the citadel on the Capitoline Hill, and only went home after the Romans paid them a large ransom. (They would have captured the citadel if not for the intervention of a manly Roman soldier and a flock of geese. Yes, I said geese.)

A Gallic Warrior
Strikes an Appropriate Pose

Naturally, most of the Romans were upset about the sack of Rome, but a guy named Marcus Camillus was particularly furious. Under his leadership, the Romans rebuilt their city and subdued the other

Latins, who had gotten uppity when Rome was in ruins. Meanwhile, even though Camillus, a patrician, was not much fonder of uppity plebeians than he was of uppity Latins, he and the other patricians came to realize that civil discord wasn't helping Rome in her external relations. So the patricians eventually made some more concessions to the plebeians, the most significant being an agreement that plebeians could be consuls.

This concession was of particular value to rich plebeians, who were increasing in number, although the average plebeian remained working class. Naturally, these rich plebeians were the ones who wanted political rights commensurate with their wealth. The average poor plebeian farmer or artisan wasn't interested in taking time off from his work to run for an office that he wasn't going to win anyway.

Anyway, as the fourth century progressed, Rome became a lot more peaceful internally. Power slowly passed into the hands of the Senate (a Latin term meaning "old guys"), which consisted mostly of ex-magistrates. In other words, the Senate included members of patrician families and members of wealthy, politically successful plebeian families. The poor people didn't complain too much, because with its newfound internal peace, Rome was now able to conquer lots of neighbors and make their land available for settlement by rich and poor alike.

Unsurprisingly, many of the neighbors objected to being conquered. In addition, when formerly friendly neighbors saw how powerful Rome was getting, they got scared of being conquered themselves. So a bunch of wars ensued, most notably against the Samnites (similar to Sabines) of mountainous inland central Italy. By the year 282 BC, the Romans had won almost all of these wars and found themselves in control of Latium, Etruria, and Samnium, as well as Campania, a region southeast of Rome that was inhabited by Greeks and Samnites.

Some of the Greeks even further southeast, notably in the city of Tarentum, were rather perturbed by the growth of Roman power. "What we need," they said (but in Greek, not in English), "is a new warrior, a flame that will drive these Romans back like sheep fleeing a large and vicious dog. Such as a mastiff, or an Irish wolfhound. Definitely not a poodle." So they invited a semi-Greek king named Pyrrhus, who lived near what is now Albania, to come over to Italy and show these Romans what war was really like.

Pyrrhus brought 25,000 men and 20 elephants with him to Italy; elephants were popular in Greek warfare in those days, despite the fact that they were hard to control and sometimes stampeded through their own army. The Roman army, though, was no match for the elephants, nor for Pyrrhus' veteran troops, and Pyrrhus won battles at Heraclea (280) and Ausculum (279). But he couldn't capture fortified cities swiftly, and he couldn't recruit new men to his armies as easily as the Romans (and forget about trying to find replacement elephants when you're in southern Italy). Since the Romans just stayed in their cities and refused to surrender, Pyrrhus got bored and wandered off to Sicily. By the time he got back, in 275, there was a new Roman army, which fought and beat him at Beneventum. Disgruntled, Pyrrhus sailed home, leaving Tarentum to be conquered by Rome in 272.

Appius Claudius Caecus

Any man who gets commemorated by a brand of homemade pizza mix probably merits a mention in this history. The Claudii were a politically prominent clan of Sabine origin; throughout the history of the Roman Republic, you'll find guys named Claudius getting elected to important public offices. Appius Claudius Caecus was a patrician and two-time consul who, depending on which modern historian you believe, was pro-plebeian, anti-plebeian, or somewhere in the middle. When old and blind, he made a famous speech in the Senate in which he opposed any peace negotiations with Pyrrhus, Pyrrhic victories notwithstanding. Earlier in his career, he had assured his immortality by ordering the construction of the Appian Way, the first of the famous Roman roads.

By now, almost 250 years had passed since the founding of the Roman Republic. Sensing that the next section of this chapter was going to be a long one, the Romans decided to pause and take stock of their situation. They found that they more or less controlled all of Italy south of the Po River valley (the Po River valley was still the Gauls' turf). Rome's control was largely indirect. Various peoples—Etruscans, Samnites, Campanians, Greeks—had varying degrees of local self-government, but they were bound to Rome by treaties obligating them to assist Rome in wars whenever Rome wanted them to. The local aristocracies mostly prospered under this arrangement, and Italy as a whole was largely satisfied with Rome's leadership. At the same time, Rome had planted

> Pyrrhus was eventually killed when an irate Greek woman threw a roofing tile at him and cracked his skull. Just in case you were wondering.

various colonies of Romans and other Latins at strategic points around the peninsula, just in case any allies were thinking of ignoring their treaty obligations. With respect to treaties, the Roman attitude was, "Trust, but verify." Or maybe that was Ronald Reagan.

Who're You Calling "Punic"?

While they were busy conquering most of Italy, the Romans had enjoyed friendly relations with the seafaring Carthaginians whose home was in North Africa. Carthage had been founded by immigrants from Phoenicia (modern Lebanon), so Romans called the Carthaganians "Punic," which sounds like an insult in English, but the Carthaginians didn't seem to mind it much. As for more substantive issues, the Romans weren't a naval power, and the Carthaginians weren't interested in settling on the Italian mainland, so the two sides could trade with each other and not dispute sovereignty over land or sea.

But by the year 264, having conquered the Greeks of southern Italy, Rome became interested in the Greeks just across the way in Sicily. Greeks and Carthaginians had been fighting for control over Sicily for hundreds of years, with neither side gaining total control. The Romans must have thought they could do better. So, on a rather flimsy pretext, they crossed the straits and went to war against both the Greeks and the Carthaginians. After a few Roman victories, the Greeks decided to switch to the winning team, but the Carthaginians kept fighting and successfully kept hold of a number of fortresses. So in 260, the Romans, noticing that Sicily was an island, started building big navies, which surprisingly usually defeated the Carthaginian fleets pretty easily. The Carthaginians thought this was manifestly unfair, given that they'd been a maritime power for hundreds of years, while the Romans had never even heard of Alfred Mahan. Fair or not, by 256, the Romans were able to land an army in Africa itself. But after some initial success, the invasion force was defeated by an army led by a Spartan mercenary.

After that, the Romans decided to forget about invading Africa and concentrate on conquering Sicily. Mostly due to the generalship of a Carthaginian named Hamilcar Barca, the war dragged on for another fifteen years. Eventually, though, Roman control of the sea, and Carthage's lack of money, caused the Carthaginian government to give up. Hamilcar and his army went home, and the peace treaty awarded Sicily to Rome.

Alas, no lounging for Hamilcar Barca. He and his countrymen were soon embroiled in a vicious war against their own former mercenary soldiers, who were disgruntled by the fact that Carthage didn't have enough money to pay their back salaries. While this war was going on, the Romans said, "Let's conquer Sardinia!" (which was a Carthaginian possession). By the time

Carthage had defeated the mercenaries, it found that Rome was firmly in control of Sicily, Sardinia, and Corsica, and there was nothing Carthage could do about it.

Being too weak to attack the Romans, Hamilcar decided to go attack Spain instead. "Hey, what'd we do?" asked the Spaniards, but to no avail; Hamilcar was determined to conquer them as a replacement for Carthage's lost island empire. Over the next couple of decades, he and his successors won control of most of southern Spain. Spain turned out to be a valuable possession, with lots of silver, some nice harbors, and tribesmen who were happy to join your army if you paid them.

The Romans were none too pleased by Carthage's success in Spain, but they were now busy conquering the Gauls in northern Italy, as well as the Illyrian pirates who lived on the eastern shore of the Adriatic Sea. So they made the Carthaginians promise to stay in southern Spain, and they also made an alliance with Saguntum, a coastal city in southern Spain, to keep Carthage from completely controlling the region. Carthage had plenty of other Spanish to fight, so these Roman moves didn't bother it too much.

The Ebro Treaty

The exact wording of the treaty restricting Carthage to southern Spain was preserved by reliable historians. The treaty said simply that the Carthaginian army couldn't go north of the Ebro River, in northeastern Spain. There's no evidence that it set any limits to what Rome was allowed to do, and it certainly didn't say that it would be okay for Carthage to attack Roman allies south of the Ebro. Nevertheless, many modern writers have imaginatively proclaimed that Hannibal's attack on Saguntum was perfectly okay, and Rome had no right to get upset about it. It's a good thing that none of these writers was President of the U.S. in 1948, when Stalin decided he had every right to take over West Berlin.

In 221, though, Hamilcar Barca's son Hannibal succeeded to the position of Carthaginian generalissimo in Spain. Hannibal hated Rome, mostly because his father had told him he should. Moreover, he thought he had a good plan to conquer Rome. He knew that most of the people of Italy were not Romans, and that they'd only been conquered by Rome in the last century. Therefore, he reasoned, they would welcome an invading Carthaginian army as liberators. Only how to get to Italy? The Romans had command of the sea, and it's a long way by land from Spain to Italy, with lots of mountains to cross along the way. And he couldn't leave Saguntum behind as a Roman base when he left, unless he was willing to let the Romans conquer Carthaginian Spain while he was gone.

A sensible man might have left well enough alone and concentrated on conquering inland Spain, instead of involving his country in another war with Rome at a time when Rome didn't seem particularly hostile. Hannibal, however, decided to attack Saguntum. The Romans protested, of course, but their protests were ignored, and their army was too busy in Illyria to intervene.

In the event, it took Hannibal eight months of siege operations to take Saguntum. This was not a good sign: if it took eight months to capture a podunk city like Saguntum, how on earth was he going to capture a metropolis like Rome? But it was too late to turn back now, since the Romans had finally declared war and were sending an army to Spain, and another one to Africa.

Hannibal was not about to wait around for the Romans to attack him. Leaving his brother Hasdrubal behind with enough troops to defend against the Romans, he took the rest of his army and marched across the Pyrenees and out of Spain forever. The Romans almost caught him on the way across what is now southern France, but he gave them the slip, fought his way through unfriendly Gallic tribes, and crossed the Alps into northern Italy.

And yes, he brought elephants with him. This is possibly the most famous thing that Hannibal did, bringing elephants across the Alps. There was even a parade on *The Simpsons* commemorating this achievement, much to Sideshow Bob's chagrin. But some people will tell you that he (Hannibal, not Sideshow Bob) didn't succeed (Sideshow Bob, in fact, did not succeed, but then, he never does), that it was too cold in the mountains, and the elephants fell off the footpaths, or got scared off by mice, or so on. Quite the contrary—Hannibal got all of his elephants across by autumn of 218 BC. He even used them in a battle at the River Trebia, against the army that, instead of going to Africa, had been diverted to northern Italy to oppose the invasion. (But Rome still sent an army to Spain, which turned out to be a good plan). The elephants were very effective against the Roman cavalry, because untrained horses are scared of elephants. The Carthaginians won the battle, but then winter came, and winter gets pretty cold in northern Italy. Too cold for the elephants, all but one of whom died.

A Worried Elephant Contemplates
Spending the Winter in Northern Italy

Elephants or no elephants, when spring came, Hannibal marched south towards Etruria, accompanied by a lot of Gauls who'd joined his army. The Etruscans, though, didn't seem very interested in helping to overthrow Rome, so the army left Etruria and went east into the mountains. A new Roman army hastened in pursuit, too hastily, as it turned out. The Carthaginians ambushed the Romans on the shores of Lake Trasimene and wiped them out. Then they marched south to try to drum up support there.

Alas, no support was forthcoming. What came forth instead in 216 was a great big Roman army, somewhere between 50,000 and 80,000 men, led by both consuls at once. Could Hannibal possibly defeat such an enormous army? Of course, because if he hadn't defeated it, he wouldn't be so famous, and you wouldn't be reading about his exploits at such length. The battle took place at Cannae, a village in southern Italy, in August 216, and when it was over only 14,000 Romans had escaped death or capture.

After Cannae, many of the peoples of southern Italy switched to Hannibal's team, and soon the Greeks of Sicily did likewise. But just as they had done with Pyrrhus, the Romans obstinately refused to surrender, and they also wisely refused to fight another major battle. Instead, they concentrated on skirmishing to wear down Hannibal's army, and on besieging disaffected cities while Hannibal's army was elsewhere. Year after year, Hannibal's strength diminished, and by 203 he had been penned into a small area in the toe of Italy, across from Sicily.

Meanwhile, a young Roman general named Publius Cornelius Scipio had been conquering Spain from Hannibal's brother Hasdrubal and an assortment of other Carthaginian generals (one of whom, confusingly, was also named Hasdrubal). He finished things up in Spain by 206, then got himself elected consul for 205. Not satisfied with having just three names, despite the fact that many Romans had only two names, while Romulus had only had one, Scipio decided to invade Africa in hopes of earning the nickname Africanus. I suppose he might also have been motivated a desire to end the war. Anyway, by 202 he had the Carthaginians ready to surrender, but then Hannibal, having finally realized that Italy was no longer the place to be, showed up with his army. "Ha!" said the Carthaginians. "Now we'll show this punk kid" (Scipio was still in his early thirties). The two armies then fought a battle at a place called Zama, which, by the way, would be a good name for a female rap artist. To the Carthaginians' great surprise, Scipio won a decisive victory. Everyone in Carthage realized then that the jig was up, even though nobody was exactly sure what a jig was. So in 201, the peace treaty was signed. Carthage became a second-rate power, Spain was confirmed as a Roman possession, and Scipio got his nickname.

Many years later, long after Scipio was dead, he got a fifth name, Major "the Elder," to distinguish him from another Publius Cornelius Scipio Africanus, who was called Minor "the Younger." No doubt Scipio was overjoyed to get a posthumous fifth name, but that's a story for another chapter. The point here is that this chapter, which has been going on for a while, is finally over, and maybe now we can all get some rest.

Western Mediterranean League Punic War Standings (201 BC)			
	W	L	T
Rome	2	0	0
Carthage	0	2	0

A Note about Names

Neither the Romans nor the Carthaginians displayed much verve when naming their children, at least not in the upper classes. Roman men normally had a personal name, like Publius, a clan name, like Cornelius, and sometimes a third name such as Scipio. As we've seen, some Romans got greedy and added one or more extra names, often nicknames; eventually, Roman emperors ended up with about as many names as members of the British royal family. But you'll notice in this book that prominent Roman men of the republican period almost all have one of a small set of personal names, such as Marcus, Publius, Servius, Gaius—no more than fifteen to choose from. Girls, on the other hand, didn't get individual names at all. If Publius Cornelius Scipio had three daughters, all of them were named Cornelia. Reminds me of boxer and grilling entrepreneur George Foreman, who named all of his sons George.

But at least you can tell Roman nobles apart by their second, and sometimes third names. Carthaginians had only one name apiece (Barca was a nickname, meaning "Lightning," applied to Hamilcar but not to his sons). The problem is that prominent Carthaginians, like prominent Romans, seem to have had maybe ten to fifteen personal names to choose from. The most common were probably Hasdrubal, Mago, Hanno, and Hannibal. During the Punic War in Spain, there were three main Carthaginian generals, one of whom was named Mago. The other two were Hasdrubal, son of Hamilcar Barca, and Hasdrubal, son of Gisco. And the Carthaginian generalissimo in Spain who immediately preceded Hannibal was yet another Hasdrubal, who happened to be Hamilcar's son-in-law. I.e., Hasdrubal son of Hamilcar was brother-in-law to Hasdrubal son-in-law of Hamilcar.

Confused? A final warning: Publius Cornelius Scipio Africanus Minor will end up fighting yet another Hasdrubal next chapter.

Review Questions for Chapter One

1. How significant was Etruscan influence on the development of early Rome?

2. *Essay question.* Should Hannibal have marched on Rome after his great victory at Cannae?

3. Can you think of anything interesting that Ancus Marcius ever did?

4. Do you think there was too much about elephants in this chapter?

5. *Bonus question.* Have you ever eaten pizza made from Appian Way® homemade pizza mix? Was it any good?

Answers to #1-#4 at bottom of page.

Answers

1) $t=2.147$, $p < .05$.

2) No.

3) Neither can I.

4) Too bad. I like elephants.

Dramatic Interlude

Time: 197 BC. Place: Cynoscephalae, in northern Greece.

Gaius and Lucius, Roman soldiers, are standing facing a range of hills, behind which is the left flank of the Macedonian army of King Philip V. To Gaius and Lucius' left and right, identically armed Roman soldiers stand waiting.

LUCIUS: Sounds like they're already engaged on the other flank. Won't be long now before we start moving.

GAIUS: I still say this is stupid. No sooner did we sign the peace treaty with Carthage than we declared war on Macedonia. And now you and I are going into battle when I should be at home tending my olive trees.

LUCIUS: If we hadn't invaded Macedonia, they would have invaded us, and just imagine what a Macedonian army would have done to your olive trees. Don't you remember how King Philip declared war on us in the middle of the 2nd Punic War?

GAIUS: And did he invade Italy? No, he did not. We sent a little army over here to oppose him, and after ten rather uneventful years, both sides agreed to call it a draw.

LUCIUS: Yeah, but then he... *Lucius pauses as a wounded velite (a lightly-armed Roman youth who fights as a skirmisher) stumbles past, an arrow sticking out of his chest.*

LUCIUS: ...then he started attacking our friends in Greece.

GAIUS: Friends in Greece? I don't have any friends in Greece. All my friends are in Italy, which is where we belong. To hell with the Greeks, that's my opinion.

LUCIUS: That's awfully shortsighted of you. Even Scipio says—

GAIUS: Enough with the Scipio references, already. Just because you served under him in Africa, you think he's Jupiter's gift to Rome. If you ask me, Scipio's just another decadent Greek-loving noble. Cato, now there's a senator for you.

LUCIUS: Who, Marcus Porcius Cato? That nobody from a small Italian town? Without a single ancestor who served as consul?

GAIUS: Yes, Cato. He knows we've got better things to do then get tangled up in the Greek east. It's not like Spain and northern Italy are pacified yet.

LUCIUS: Which is exactly why we've got to take on Philip before he gets too powerful. Let him conquer Greece, and soon he'll be marching into northern Italy, and all the Gauls will rally to him.

GAIUS: Yeah, sure. All I know is, my idiot brother-in-law is running my farm while I'm stuck out here. By the time I get back, he'll have me so far in debt that I'll have to sell my land to some rich noble and become a landless proletarian.

Just then, a trumpet sounds, a drumbeat begins, and a centurion's voice is heard offstage.

CENTURION: All right, lads, here we go. Take it easy now, no running. And don't throw your javelins before I give the word.

GAIUS (*resignedly*): I guess it's all academic now. Well, let's go, see, and conquer.

Gaius, Lucius, and their silent cohorts hoist their shields and exeunt omnes, stage left, marching in time with the drum, which continues to beat as the stage goes dark.

THE HISTORY OF ROME

Chapter Two

in which the Romans, by spreading their dominion east and west, but not north or south, force us to rotate this page 90 degrees so as to fit the map on it, and further cause us to orient the text of the chapter in the same way for the sake of consistency, and also because the usual orientation gets kind of boring after a while, and a little change might be nice

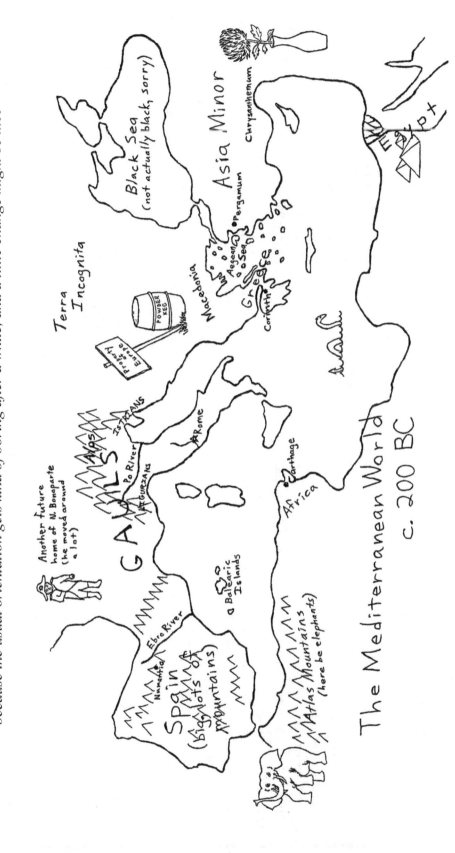

The Mediterranean World
c. 200 BC

A Lot of Wars

Many a nation, having spent the last several centuries engaged in nearly constant warfare, would have taken a rest after so fierce a struggle as the 2nd Punic War. But not the Romans! As you know from the dramatic interlude preceding this chapter, they leapt right into a war with King Philip V of Macedonia. Exactly why they did so isn't clear. It couldn't have been just the desire to keep fighting, because there were still plenty of Gauls and Spanish to conquer. Probably the main reason was that the Romans didn't want any one power to win control of Greece, since a united Greece could be a threat to Rome. So Rome declared war, defeated Philip at the battle of Cynoscephalae, and made him give up his fleet and withdraw his forces from the cities of Greece proper. Then the Romans, who didn't want the hassle of ruling Greece themselves, returned to Italy, announcing as they did so that the Greeks were now free.

Unfortunately, various Greeks and other easterners thought that "freedom" meant freedom to make alliances, fight wars, and try to gain the sort of hegemony in the Aegean Sea area that Rome had achieved in Italy. In other words, they were missing the whole point of the 2nd Macedonian War. So the Romans, despite being busy fighting in northern Italy and Spain, kept finding themselves sending another army to explain things to the latest confused Greek person.

One person who got confused was Antiochus the Great, a king of Macedonian descent who ruled over most of the Middle East. Antiochus had recently fought successful wars against the Parthians (in what is now Iran) and the Ptolemaic kingdom of Egypt, thus earning his nickname. Now he thought the time was ripe to move from Asia Minor into Greece. However, after an encounter with a Roman army at the battle of Thermopylae in 191 BC, he decided that the time was ripe to go back to Asia Minor. Unfortunately for Antiochus, the Romans, having determined that he was not so great after all, followed him and crushed his army at a place called Magnesia, in 189 BC. The Roman general at Magnesia was the consul Lucius Cornelius Scipio, Africanus' little brother. Africanus was helping Lucius out with the war but was out sick on the day of the battle.

By the terms of the peace treaty, Antiochus agreed to stay out of Asia Minor altogether. Antiochus died right after the war ended, and the Scipio brothers probably wished that they had too, because when they got home to Rome they were promptly put on trial on suspicion of embezzlement and bribe-taking. At least Lucius was put on trial—whether Africanus was actually charged is not completely clear. At any rate, Lucius had to pay a fine, although a helpful tribune saved him from going to prison. Africanus was not convicted of anything, but, feeling unappreciated, he retired to his country estate and died soon afterward.

What about Hannibal?

Maybe one reason that Antiochus decide to attack the Romans was that Hannibal, whom the Romans had ordered to leave Carthage, was now hanging around Antiochus' court, giving him advice. Sound advice, no doubt, like, "Go ahead, fight the Romans! Maybe it won't end in a disastrous defeat and the cession of a huge and valuable chunk of your territory." When, in fact, the war did end in a disastrous defeat for Antiochus, one of the terms of the peace treaty was that he was supposed to hand Hannibal over to the Romans. But the wily Carthaginian had already slipped off to the court of Prusias of Bithynia, a little kingdom in northwest Asia Minor. Prusias employed Hannibal as a general for a while, but in 183 he gave way under Roman pressure and agreed to surrender Hannibal to them. Unable to escape this time, Hannibal committed suicide.

The man principally responsible for the trial was Marcus Porcius Cato, a politician of humble background who had made himself popular by being grumpy. Among the things that made Cato grumpy were: women who liked nice clothes and jewelry; Roman officials who oppressed people in the provinces; slaves who complained about being worked to death; people named Scipio; statues; and Greeks of any sort. Cato had fought in the 2nd Punic War and had served as consul in 195; during his consulship he conducted successful military campaigns in Spain. After the trial of the Scipios, he was elected censor, an important job which allowed him to throw people out of the Senate if they annoyed him. He also got to make rules intended to limit how much people spent on things like clothes and home furnishings, but the Romans mostly said, "Those are great rules, Cato! Just what we need in our decadent society!" and then went on spending their money however they saw fit. Cato is one of the most famous of the early Romans, and if you want to read more about him, you can consult a book called *My World and Welcome to It*, by James Thurber. Thurber's book includes Cato's magical formula for warding off sprains.

Meanwhile, back in the Greek east, the main beneficiary of Rome's wars turned out to be Rome's ally

Cato's Nightmare

Pergamum, which became the dominant power in Asia Minor once Antiochus left. King Philip of Macedonia wisely refrained from provoking the Romans while he rebuilt his country's strength. But in the 170's, the efforts of Philip's son and successor Perseus to win friends and influence people in Greece made King Eumenes II of Pergamum nervous. He told the Romans they better do something about Perseus, so the Romans obligingly declared war in 171. Perseus put up a surprisingly good fight against fairly mediocre Roman generals, but in 168, Rome sent out a competent general named Lucius Aemilius Paullus. When their armies met at the battle of Pydna in that same year, Perseus, lacking the Medusa head which had helped out his mythological namesake, was resoundingly defeated.

The Romans were getting sick of fighting Macedonian Wars, so they decided to exile Perseus to a Roman-owned island and break Macedonia up into four separate republics. Also, suspecting that a lot of the Greeks had secretly been rooting for Perseus, they executed some of them and took others, including the historian Polybius, as hostages back to Italy. By this time, the Gauls of northern Italy had been subdued, along with the Ligurians and Istrians who lived on the western and eastern borders of northern Italy, respectively.

Many of the Spanish were still resisting Roman rule, but the Romans didn't care enough to make a big deal about it. Farther afield, both Antiochus' successors and their traditional enemies, the Ptolemaic kings of Egypt, were too weak to threaten Rome. So everything appeared to be hunky-dory, to use a technical term, on the international front, while on the domestic front, the plunder from successful wars was making lots of Romans wealthy.

But Cato was still alive, and now that he was old he was grumpier than ever. After a visit to Carthage in about 153 BC, he got worried that Carthage was getting too prosperous, and he started going around saying "Carthage must be destroyed!" all the time. A member of the Scipio family, Scipio Nasica by name, disagreed, so he started going around saying "Carthage must be preserved!"

win the war quickly. Remembering what had worked in the last Punic War, they decided to look for a young guy named Scipio who could be appointed general. As it happened, Scipio Africanus' elder son, having no sons of his own, had adopted one of Aemilius Paullus' sons. The adoptee had changed his name to Publius Cornelius Scipio, but with Aemilianus tacked on to show who his natural father was. And so the auspiciously-named young Publius Cornelius Scipio Aemilianus was sent to Africa, where he captured and destroyed Carthage in the year 146 BC, thus lengthening his name to Publius Cornelius Scipio Aemilianus Africanus Minor.

146 turned out to be a good year for destroying major cities. While the 3rd Punic War was going on, the Macedonians had decided that they didn't like being divided into four separate republics, so one of them pronounced himself king and started the 4th Macedonian War. He was quickly defeated, but meanwhile some of the Greeks, unruly as ever, had turned anti-Roman. So in 146, the Roman army in Macedonia marched into Greece, destroyed Corinth, and shipped Corinth's treasure back to Rome. The rest of the Greeks decided that maybe it was time to stop being so unruly.

Did Rome have a three-strikes-and-you're-out policy? You be the judge. Carthage's record in wars with Rome was 0-3; Macedonia's was 0-3-1 (the first war having been a draw). Now both Macedonia and the Carthaginian parts of Africa became Roman provinces. Once again, things seemed to be both hunky and dory.

Except for Spain. Like a nagging sore, or a pesky dog, or, to use Napoleon's term, a bleeding ulcer, the Spanish problem just wouldn't go away. It turned out that Spain was full of mountains, as well as being pretty big, neither of which facts the Romans had fully comprehended before they started trying to conquer the country. Also, unlike the Greek east, it wasn't full of

---

Polybius

Polybius, whose name means "lots of life," was a Greek statesman who was deported to Rome in 167 BC. This turned out to be a good thing in the long run, because he ended up being a friend and mentor to Scipio Aemilianus. He accompanied Scipio on some of the latter's campaigns, and he later wrote a 'history of Rome and the Mediterranean from 264 to 146 BC. Polybius was a good historian but not much of a prose stylist, so his history wasn't particularly popular, meaning that most of it has been lost.

On a more personal note, his name turned out to be accurate in that he supposedly lived to be 82 years old, dying in 118 BC when he fell off of his horse.

Cato won the argument eventually: in 149, a few months before Cato finally kicked the bucket at age 85, Rome announced the start of the 3rd Punic War (tickets available at the box office, five sesterces for bleacher seats, ten sesterces for the bandstand).

To everyone's surprise, Carthage put up a good fight, to no one's surprise, under the leadership of a man named, to no one's surprise, Hasdrubal. The Romans were very embarrassed by their failure to

Trouble at Home

Whenever the Romans conquered some foreign country, they acquired a lot of (1) land confiscated from their former enemies, which normally became public land available for private exploitation; (2) liquid assets, in the form of plunder and tribute/taxation; and (3) captives who could be sold into slavery. In other words, conquest ensured that land and slaves were cheap, and money was plentiful. It thus became possible for wealthy Romans to have large agricultural estates worked by harshly-treated slaves, not just in Italy, but also in provinces like Sicily. This was bad for Roman peasant farmers, who couldn't compete effectively with these agribusinesses, and often ended up having to sell their farms to one of the agribusinessmen. The new system wasn't so great for the slaves either, of course, and in fact the slaves of Sicily revolted in the 130's. However, the Roman government believed, correctly as it turned out, that the slave revolt could be stamped out by the brutal application of force, without any attention to the underlying causes of the rebellion.

Dealing with dispossessed Roman peasants was a little less straightforward, given that they were Roman citizens, so it was illegal to just kill them. Many of them moved to Rome, hoping to get work of some sort, or to become clients of a rich guy. Clients supported their patrons politically, in return for the same sort of help and protection that big-city bosses used to give to immigrant voters in the U.S. But the landless urbanites on the whole remained poor and disgruntled.

In the year 133, while Scipio Aemilianus was off earning the nickname Numantinus, his relative Tiberius Sempronius Gracchus came up with a plan to regruntle the urban poor. It involved establishing an agrarian commission to distribute public land to impoverished city dwellers. Gracchus wasn't motivated purely by altruism; by law, only men who met a minimum

precious art and other valuable merchandise that made it fun to plunder if you were a Roman. So not too many Romans wanted to fight in Spain, and various wars persisted for decades.

Like the earlier situation at Carthage, the Spanish situation eventually came to be seen as an embarrassment by many Romans, so they finally asked Scipio Africanus Minor if he'd be willing to take charge of the fighting. "Can I have another nickname?" he asked. "Only if you win," was the reply. So he did win, by capturing (and destroying) the enemy stronghold of Numantia in 133 BC, whereupon he became known as, if you can believe it, Publius Cornelius Scipio Aemilianus Africanus Minor Numantinus, or "Bud" to his friends.

Also in 133, Eumenes II's son King Attalus III of Pergamum died, and in his will it turned out that he had bequeathed his kingdom to Rome. This was kind of an odd bequest, but the Romans had gotten used to plundering the east, so they accepted the bequest and turned Pergamum into a Roman province named Asia. Thus, by the late 2nd century, Rome was the dominant power not just in the western Mediterranean, but all over the Mediterranean world. One could easily assume that success overseas had led to happy times at home, unless, indeed, one had read the title of the next section of this chapter, which you should do now if you haven't done so already.

A Pesky
Spanish Dog

property requirement were supposed to serve in the army, so a lack of peasant farmers meant a lack of soldiers. However, many senators had occupied extremely large chunks of public land for generations, effectively incorporating them into their personal agricultural estates, so they did their best to block Gracchus' plan. Gracchus therefore resorted to arguably illegal measures to get his way. "Tut tut," said the senators, "we can't have people resorting to illegality," so they got together a mob of their clients and killed Gracchus and a bunch of his followers.

Even with Gracchus dead, the agrarian commission that he had established survived. It ran into trouble, though, because only Romans were allowed to get land. Non-Roman Italians, loyal allies for over a century, were in fact thrown off the land to make way for Romans, which was technically legal but didn't make the Italians very happy. Then Scipio Aemilianus, who got back to Rome after Gracchus' death and wasn't too pleased with what Gracchus had done, used his influence to limit the commission's powers. When Scipio died unexpectedly in 129 BC, some people suspected that he had been murdered by the Gracchans to get him out of the way.

Meanwhile, it turned out that land reform was making only a small dent in urban poverty. So now everyone was disgruntled: the Italians because they lacked the benefits of Roman citizenship; the senators because their authority had been challenged; and the poor people because they were still poor. Affairs drifted along uneasily for a while, until Tiberius Gracchus' younger brother Gaius got himself elected tribune in 123.

Gaius had a more wide-ranging reform plan than his brother. To pass it, he needed support from the so-called equites or knights, a class of non-senatorial businessmen who had grown increasingly rich and influential at Rome as Rome's empire grew. The equites' main political interest was in being allowed to get rich by exploiting the provinces without any regard for ethical business practices. Gaius therefore passed some laws to help them out, and he also passed laws to (1) restore full power to the agrarian commission, (2) spend money on job-providing public works like road-building, (3) establish agricultural colonies overseas for poor Romans to settle at, and (4) provide grain at below-market prices to the urban proletariat. Gaius passed these laws by taking them directly to the popular assembly, without seeking approval from the Senate. This was the sort of unorthodox technique that had gotten his brother killed, but having wider political support than Tiberius, Gaius got away with it.

Re-elected to the tribuneship for 122, Gaius now proposed to give citizenship to some of the Italians and increased rights to the rest of them. This turned out to be a mistake, because Romans rich and poor were opposed to doing anything to help out non-Romans. Gaius was not re-elected tribune for 121. In an angry mood, he and some of his followers gathered on the Aventine Hill, perhaps with insurrectionary intent. The Senate, which had experience dealing with testy Gracchi, passed a decree urging the consuls to take steps to preserve public order by any means

---

Knights in Shining Armor?

The Latin word *equites* means "horsemen," and back in the early days it had designated those citizens who weren't in the senatorial class, but were still rich enough to own warhorses, and thus to fight as cavalrymen rather than infantry in the Roman army. So they were vaguely similar to the knights of the Middle Ages, and it used to be traditional to translate *equites* as "knights." But to modern people, that term summons up images of dragons and damsels in distress, whereas the *equites* of late republican Rome had more in common with Citibank than with Sir Lancelot. So it's common nowadays to simply use the term equites in English, or sometimes equestrians.

necessary. "Any means?" asked a consul, dragging a finger across his throat. "Yes, any means," said the senators, pantomiming the throwing of rocks and javelins. So the consul gathered some troops and killed Gracchus and most of his supporters.

Whew! The Senate breathed a sigh of relief. Then, showing that it had very little interest in remedying the causes of all this trouble, it abolished the agrarian commission, abandoned the colonization plan, and ignored the Italians' pleas for better treatment. But the equites kept their privileges, and the urban poor kept getting subsidized grain, so there wasn't a revolution.

While Gaius-related activities were in full swing at Rome, some Roman generals, noticing that there were parts of the western Mediterranean that hadn't been conquered yet, took over the Balearic Islands (123 BC) and the strip of coastline between Spain and northern Italy (121 BC), in what is now southern France. Since the inhabitants of this strip of coastline, apart from the Greeks in the cities, were mostly Gauls, the Romans called their new province Transalpine Gaul, i.e., "Gaul across the Alps," and they named northern Italy Cisalpine Gaul, or "Gaul on this side of the Alps." Imaginative people, those Romans. They also divided Spain into two provinces, called Closer Spain and Farther Away Spain. Guess which one was closer to Italy.

Looking at the map, the Romans had good cause to feel satisfied with the state of their state, the dominant country in the world as they knew it. Taking a look at the social situation at home would have been considerably less satisfying, so most Romans spent as much time as possible looking at maps, and as little time as possible doing sociological research. You should therefore follow their example and take a look at the map below, which makes a nice ending point for this chapter.

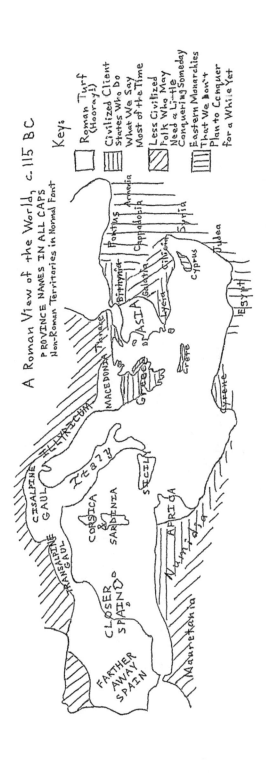

A Roman View of the World, c. 115 BC
PROVINCE NAMES IN ALL CAPS
Non-Roman Territories in Normal Font

Key:
- Roman Turf (Hooray!)
- Civilized Client States Who Do What We Say Most of the Time
- Less Civilized Folk Who May Need a Little Conquering Someday
- Eastern Monarchies That We Don't Plan to Conquer for a While Yet

A Family Affair

Roman politics in the middle Republic was dominated by a small number of noble families whose ancestors had previously attained the consulship. Magistrates of all sorts tended to come from these families, or from other families which allied themselves to the great houses. It was unusual for any one man to hold the consulship more than once or twice, but the Senate as a whole, which set most state policies, pretty much followed the lead of the ex-consuls among its membership. So a lot of consulships shows that a family was particularly influential.

If a new man, like Cato, rose to prominence, he was typically co-opted into the system by marriage alliances. Thus, Cato's son Marcus married Aemilius Paullus' daughter, and although Marcus himself died in 152 BC without becoming consul, Cato's grandsons Marcus and Gaius attained the consulship in 118 and 114 respectively.

The chart below shows some, but by no means all, of the patterns of intermarriage and other relationships involving the Scipio family. It's worth noting that family ties weren't necessarily a guarantee of political co-operation. The leader of the senatorial mob that killed Tiberius Gracchus was Tiberius' first cousin, Scipio Nasica Serapio. Scipio Aemilianus, who was Tiberius' brother-in-law, first cousin by adoption, and first cousin once removed by blood, nevertheless approved of Tiberius' murder.

In the chart, the date in parentheses indicates the year(s), if any, in which the indicated person held the consulship. Male first names are abbreviated as follows: C.=Gaius, Cn.=Gnaeus, L.=Lucius, M.=Marcus, P.=Publius, Ti.=Tiberius.

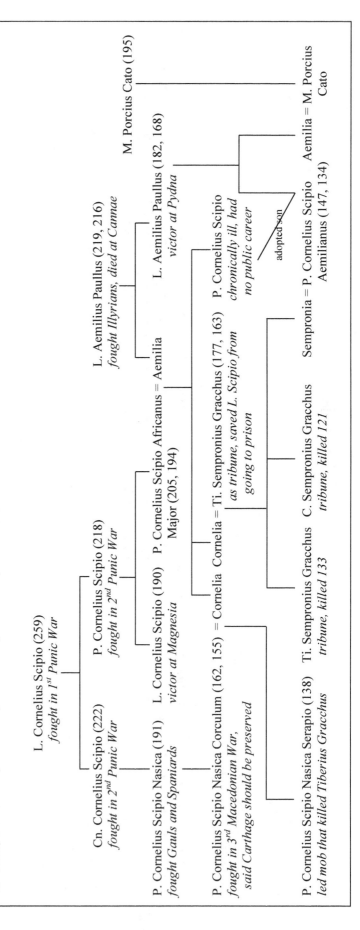

L. Cornelius Scipio (259)
fought in 1st Punic War

P. Cornelius Scipio (218)
fought in 2nd Punic War

Cn. Cornelius Scipio (222)
fought in 2nd Punic War

L. Cornelius Scipio (190)
victor at Magnesia

P. Cornelius Scipio Africanus = Aemilia
Major (205, 194)

L. Aemilius Paullus (219, 216)
fought Illyrians, died at Cannae

L. Aemilius Paullus (182, 168)
victor at Pydna

M. Porcius Cato (195)

P. Cornelius Scipio Nasica (191)
fought Gauls and Spaniards

P. Cornelius Scipio Nasica Corculum (162, 155) = Cornelia   Cornelia = Ti. Sempronius Gracchus (177, 163)
fought in 3rd Macedonian War,   *as tribune, saved L. Scipio from*
said Carthage should be preserved   *going to prison*

P. Cornelius Scipio
chronically ill, had
no public career

Sempronia = P. Cornelius Scipio
Aemilianus (147, 134)

Aemilia = M. Porcius
Cato

adopted son

P. Cornelius Scipio Nasica Serapio (138)
led mob that killed Tiberius Gracchus

Ti. Sempronius Gracchus
tribune, killed 133

C. Sempronius Gracchus
tribune, killed 121

22

Discussion Questions for Chapter Two
no answers provided

1. Why does Napoleon Bonaparte keep showing up in this history, while important Romans such as Fabius Maximus have not been mentioned at all?

2.a) Why did Scipio Aemilianus like destroying cities so much? Did it have anything to do with the fact that his father divorced his mother and gave him up for adoption?

   b) Did you believe me when I claimed that Scipio Aemilianus' friends called him "Bud"? If so, I have a bridge I'd like to sell you.

3. It is customary, almost obligatory, for histories of Rome to have chapter breaks in the years 264 BC and 133 BC. This history, instead, has chapter breaks in the year 201-200 BC and somewhere around 120-115 BC. Can you think of a good explanation for why the chapter breaks in this history are in the wrong place? If so, please let me know.

4.a) If you were an urbanite who was given a small plot of land far away from your family and friends, in an economic climate that made it very hard for small farmers to compete with large-scale agricultural enterprises, how many years of backbreaking toil would it take before you sold your land to a noble and moved back to Rome, or joined the army, or something?

   b) Explain why the Gracchan agrarian commission was not quite so successful as the Gracchi had hoped it would be.

23

Musical Interlude

Below are the lyrics to the campaign theme song that Gaius Gracchus used when he ran for the tribunate. He sang it frequently, to the delight of his supporters. I guess he had a nice voice.

I dreamed I saw T.G. last night
Alive as you and me,
Says I, "But bro, you're ten years dead,"
"I never died," says he, "I never died," says he.

"Right here in Rome," says I to him,
Him standing by my bed,
"They lynched you 'cause you helped the poor,"
Says he, "But I ain't dead," says he, "But I ain't dead."

"The Senate bosses got you, bro,
They killed you, bro," says I,
"Takes more than clubs to kill a man,"
Says he, "I didn't die," says he, "I didn't die."

And standing there as big as life
And chuckling in his throat,
He says, "One thing they didn't kill,
The power of the vote, the power of the vote."

"T.G. ain't dead," he says to me,
"T.G. ain't never died,
Where Roman poor have need of land,
T.G. is at their side, T.G. is at their side."

"From Palatine to Aventine,
From sea to shining sea,
Where Romans fight for land reform,"
Says he, "You'll find T.G.," says he, "You'll find T.G."

(with apologies to Alfred Hayes)

THE HISTORY OF ROME

Chapter Three

*in which a surprisingly large amount of stuff happens,
considering how short the chapter is*

*and for which we don't need a new map, since the map at the end
of the last chapter covers everything in this one, so instead of a map, here's a picture of
Germanic tribespeople wandering through Switzerland*

How Do You Say "Déja Vu" in Latin?

Although the next several decades were pretty exciting, they also get kind of repetitive at times. We'll go through them quickly; see if you can spot repetition anywhere.

In the year 113, a wandering horde of Germanic barbarians called Cimbri and Teutones bumped into a Roman army in northern Illyricum. The Germans won the battle, but then they wandered off into Switzerland, possibly because they liked skiing.

In the year 112, Rome got involved in a war with a Numidian king named Jugurtha, who had massacred some Italian merchants. The Senate appointed one of the consuls to fight the war, but he made slow progress. Wanting a different general, the people elected a new man named Gaius Marius as consul. Marius raised a large army by eliminating the minimum property requirement for enlistment.

The Cimbri and Teutones reappeared west of Switzerland and defeated armies led by consuls in the years 109 and 107. Then they wandered around Gaul for a while.

Marius eventually defeated the Numidians but was unable to capture Jugurtha, who was hiding out in Mauretania. An officer of Marius', Lucius Cornelius Sulla by name, talked the king of Mauretania into handing Jugurtha over to him, and then annoyed Marius by taking credit for winning the war.

In 105, the Cimbri and Teutones crushed a Roman army at the battle of Arausio in Transalpine Gaul. After the battle, the Cimbri and Teutones chose to wander around Spain and Gaul for a while.

Arausio was Rome's most disastrous defeat since Cannae. Wanting a new general, the Roman people elected Marius consul. He created a large army by enrolling lots of people who didn't meet the old minimum property requirement. Then he defeated the Cimbri and Teutones in separate battles in 102 and 101, when they were trying to wander into Italy.

At the same time as Marius was killing Germans, there was another slave revolt in Sicily. But the Romans figured, correctly, that they could crush the revolt through the use of military force, without worrying about the causes of the rebellion.

Meanwhile, at Rome, a tribune named Saturninus was agitating for reforms, including giving cheap grain and free land to poor Romans. Since he couldn't get everything he wanted through legal means, he resorted to violence. In response, the Senate passed a decree advising the consuls to preserve the state by any means necessary. Then anti-reform senators got a mob together and killed Saturninus. Marius, who couldn't make up his mind which side he was on, lost credibility with everyone and wandered off to the provinces.

Also around this time, the Senate decided to make Cilicia a province so that pirates would stop using it as a base. A few years later, Sulla was sent out to govern the new province, and while there he got into a minor squabble with King Mithridates of Pontus over control of a neighboring kingdom. The squabble ended with Mithridates agreeing to go home to Pontus and to be less disruptive in the future.

What about Women?

By now, alert readers will have noticed that women have not been particularly prominent in this history. Sorry about that. But this is an old-fashioned political and military history, not a social history of the type that came into vogue in the late 20th century. It happens that the Romans, like most ancient people, didn't think that women should have any part in public affairs. Behind the scenes, of course, mothers, sisters, wives, and daughters of leading politicians may well have had some influence, but it's hard to gauge at this distance. In any case, Roman women never became magistrates or generals themselves, which is the main way of getting yourself mentioned in this book. A female consul—that would really have made Cato grumpy.

In the mid 90's, a king of Cyrene named Ptolemy Apion died, and it turned out that he had bequeathed his kingdom to Rome in his will. The Romans accepted the bequest but didn't bother to install a provincial government for another couple of decades.

In 92, a tribune named Drusus agitated for reforms. He wanted to give land to poor Romans and citizenship to Italians. Resorting to violence to get his way, he was assassinated.

The Italians promptly rebelled against Rome, thus starting a war which was *the* social event of the next few seasons. Marius, who had wandered back to Italy, fought against the Italians, but he wasn't as successful as Sulla and another general named Pompeius Strabo. Sulla annoyed Marius by taking credit for winning the war, but really none of the generals was as important to the war effort as Rome's decision, after some rough going in the first year of fighting, to give the Italians citizenship after all. This decision no doubt gratified the ghosts of those Romans and Italians who'd been killed fighting each other because Rome had refused to give the Italians citizenship.

Back in the east, Mithridates had gotten into a squabble with the Romans over control of a neighboring kingdom, and in 88 BC he massacred some Italian merchants. The Senate appointed Sulla, who was now consul, to take charge of the war against Mithridates. At the same time, a tribune named Sulpicius Rufus agitated for reforms that would give increased political power to the new Italian citizens. To get his measures passed, he resorted to violence and drove Sulla out of Rome. Then, in a bid to get Marius to support him, he also got the people to agree that they wanted a different general to go fight Mithridates, and he passed a law replacing Sulla with Marius.

Sulla, a poor man who hoped to get rich by plundering the east, had not objected too strongly to being driven out of Rome, since he was leaving soon anyway. But being deprived of the command against Mithridates was another matter: he promptly decided that as consul it was his responsibility to preserve the state by any means necessary. So he marched his army back to Rome and killed Sulpicius and a lot of his followers. He failed to kill Marius, but he drove him out of Rome. Having lost credibility, Marius took to wandering around the provinces again.

Marius, c. 87 BC

Then Sulla took his army off to fight Mithridates. Once he was gone, one of the consuls for 87, Lucius Cornelius Cinna, revived Sulpicius' proposals with regard to the Italian citizens. Everyone was confused by this, since agitating for reforms of that sort was supposed to be what tribunes did, not consuls. But eventually the Senate and the other consul, Gnaeus Octavius, decided that if Cinna was going to act like a tribune, they would treat him like one. So they got together a mob and attacked him; although they failed to kill him, they did drive him out of Rome.

Cinna figured that if Sulla, as consul, could march on Rome, then so could he. Marius wandered back to Italy, joined Cinna, and helped him to raise an army. Pompeius Strabo, who was still hanging around with the army that he had led against the Italians, couldn't make up his mind which side he was on and lost credibility, then died at a convenient moment. Cinna and Marius captured Rome, and Octavius was killed. Marius, who had gotten kind of nutty in his old age, killed some of his old political enemies but died soon afterward.

Cinna spent the next few years getting himself re-elected consul every year, which was technically illegal, but what the heck. Sulla spent the next few years driving Mithridates out of Greece and the province of Asia, which he had invaded while the Romans were too busy with other stuff to stop him. After a couple of years of fighting, Mithridates agreed to go home to Pontus and be less disruptive in the future.

Sulla now decided to march on Rome again. Cinna wanted to stop him, but he was killed by some mutinous soldiers. When Sulla reached Italy in 83, he was joined by some young anti-Cinna nobles, notably Marcus Licinius Crassus and Pompeius Strabo's son Gnaeus Pompeius. Sulla quickly captured Rome, and the young Pompeius, who's normally known in English as Pompey, drove the enemy out of Sicily and Africa. The remnants of the pro-Cinna forces gathered in Spain under the command of a general named Sertorius, but Sulla controlled everything else. Sulla's first act was to imitate Marius, but on a much larger scale, by having lots of his old political enemies killed. Then, being as bored as you are with all this repetitious violence, he decided to shake things up a bit by getting himself proclaimed dictator in 82 BC.

Proletarians of the World, Unite?

It's worth pointing out that the reformist politicians whom so many senators hated were also senators, and often members of very influential noble families. Thus, the Gracchi had consular ancestors stretching back several generations on both sides of their family, while Drusus' father had been both consul and censor. In other words, the men who cast themselves as champions of the poor and downtrodden were by no means poor and downtrodden themselves. Even slaves, when they rebelled, generally weren't interested in abolishing slavery as an institution. They just didn't want to be slaves themselves.

The Romans Learn to Take Dictation

Dictator! That made people sit up and take notice. Unless they were standing at the time, in which case, they sat down and took notice. The dictatorship was an old Roman institution, for emergency use only, whereby a single dictator, who outranked the consuls, was appointed for the duration of the emergency, but for no more than six months at most. It had been used a lot in the early days for wars against Aequi, Volsci, etc., but by Sulla's day there hadn't been a dictator for well over a century. What's more, Sulla announced that he was going to ignore the six-month limit and keep being dictator for as long as he wanted. He also announced that he was by no means done killing political enemies, since he had decided to rub out not just people who had opposed him in the past, but people whom he regarded as likely to oppose him in the future.

As it turned out, Sulla's definition of potential enemies was very broad, in part because he needed to confiscate a lot of dead enemies' property to give land to his troops. Back when military service had been restricted to landholders, discharged veterans would normally have just gone back to their own farms. Marius, by opening up the ranks to landless volunteers, had guaranteed that a great many retiring veterans had no land to go back to. Since there was no such thing as a military pension, they therefore demanded land grants as a guarantee that they wouldn't end up poor proletarians again.

So, partly to get land, Sulla published a list, called the proscription list, of several thousand people for whose death the state would pay a reward. However, not all of his enactments were motivated by greed. In fact, Sulla, who wasn't an idiot, had noticed that Rome had been having civil governance problems for several decades now. Sulla attributed these problems to the decline of the Senate's influence, a decline that he attributed to (1) unruly urban proletarians, who elected (2) impertinent tribunes, who won support from both (3) equites who would sell out to anyone for the right price and (4) Italians who wanted increased political influence. So as dictator, Sulla (1) eliminated the distribution of subsidized grain, (2) greatly reduced the power of the tribunate, (3) co-opted hundreds of leading equites into the Senate, killed a couple thousand others, and reduced the political rights of the remnant, and (4) took land away from Italians and gave it to his discharged veterans. He also made prior Senate approval obligatory for the passage of future laws. Thus, having made the Senate supreme, and having killed a few dozen senators who opposed him and packed the new Senate with his supporters, he abolished the censorship so that no one would be able to change the composition of the Senate in the future. Lastly, he passed a law designed to keep governors and army commanders from acting as independently as he had done. But he must have known that any truly successful army commander, backed by loyal veterans, would be as hard to control as Sulla himself had been in the same circumstances.

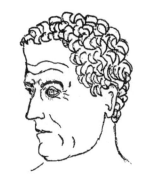

Satisfied with his work, Sulla resigned the dictatorship in late 81 and eventually left Rome for his country estate, no doubt planning to enjoy a lengthy retirement now that he had gotten rich from plundering the east. Instead, he died in 78 BC. Before his death, there were already signs of trouble for his new order. One of the consuls for 78, Marcus Aemilius Lepidus, had been elected despite Sulla's opposition to his candidacy. The Italians were grumbling about having their land confiscated. In Spain, one of Sulla's top lieutenants was proving unable to defeat Sertorius. Other top lieutenants, like Pompey and Crassus, were on bad terms with Sulla before he died.

Sulla is Satisfied

Still, the system had a good chance of working, as long as the Senate didn't need to entrust large armies to charismatic generals who, if successful, would win the undying loyalty of veteran troops who cared little for constitutional niceties. In other words, Sulla's constitution could endure as long as Rome didn't get into any major wars.

Anyone who thinks that Rome wasn't going to get into more major wars had better go back and re-read all three chapters of this book so far.

The Beginnings of Latin Literature

Rome's conquest of much of the Greek-speaking world had brought it into increasingly intimate contact with Greek culture—and I don't just mean with the prostitutes at Greek temples of Aphrodite. A Greek named Livius Andronicus, who was captured at Tarentum in 272, later translated Greek plays and Homer's *Odyssey* into Latin, and soon Romans were following his lead in both genres. History came next, and eventually philosophy, despite the efforts of traditionalists to keep philosophy out. By the 1st century BC, Rome had a rich literary tradition, although its greatest masterpieces had yet to be written. Most of the early literature has been lost between then and now, unfortunately, although we do still have some very funny plays by a guy named Plautus and some moderately funny plays by a guy named Terence. Also extant is a book on agricultural methods, written by no less a person than Cato. Cato's book is probably very interesting if you know something about farming, but it's kind of dull for people like me who grew up in the suburbs.

Discussion Questions for Chapter Three
no answers provided

1.a) If Marius and Sulla were alive today and running for the presidency of the United States, who do you think would win?
  b) What if they had a boxing match instead?
  c) A game of checkers?

2. Compare and contrast Roman land reform proposals as described in this chapter with those enacted in Denmark in 1899 and 1919.

3. *Bonus question.* Have you noticed that the chapters in this book are getting progressively shorter as we go along? Do you think that there's any meaning to this pattern?

Epistolary Interlude

Gaius Julius Caesar (who, according to the Romans, became a god after he died, just like Romulus, but didn't change his name to Quirinus or anything silly like that) was a member of a patrician, but not especially prominent family. The excerpts below are from selected letters that he wrote to an unidentified non-Roman who was his pen pal from Caesar's youth up until his late twenties. (I made these letters up. Don't go thinking they're genuine or anything.)

Written sometime in the mid-80's. Sorry to hear about the jackrabbit problem. As for myself, a lot has happened since I last wrote to you. My father died, and I became head of the family at age sixteen. Mom and I agreed that I should get married, and guess who I'm engaged to! Cornelia, daughter of Cinna, who's been consul for the past couple of years! This really opens up possibilities. My father never reached the consulship, even though Marius married his sister, my aunt Julia, as I told you in an earlier letter. But with Cinna on my side, I'm definitely on my way. And Cinna is a great man, too. Friend of the people, allied with Marius, but good at conciliating the leading senators, an excellent politician with a distinguished military record. Just the kind of clear-sighted leader Rome needs.

Of course, some people are worried that Sulla, who's off in the east fighting Mithridates, is going to come back at the head of his army and try to overthrow the government again. All I can say is that, if he does try it, we'll be more than ready. It's too bad I'm too young to get appointed an officer in the legions. I think I'd make a good general.

You might try poisoning some lettuce. Jackrabbits eat lettuce, don't they?

Written sometime around 81 BC. Sorry I haven't written for a while. I've been in hiding and am now on my way to Asia. After my father-in-law's death, things didn't go so well. Sulla came back, and a lot of nobles joined him, like that twit Pompey. (I hear that Sulla thinks Pompey is awfully conceited and has started calling him "Pompey the Great." Pompey's probably dumb enough not to recognize sarcasm when he hears it.)

The less said about the civil war, the better; the main thing is that Sulla won. Then he told me to divorce Cornelia. Hello! Just because you're dictator doesn't mean you can force me to get rid of my wife. I told him no, so he confiscated all my property, and for a while I thought he was going to put me on the proscription list. That's why I was in hiding. Now he's announced that I get to live, but I've decided to go off to the provinces for a while just in case he changes his mind.

Still, you've got to hand it to Sulla. I may not like his politics, but he doesn't worry about offending people when he thinks he's right. And he's got an army to back him up. One thing his career proves is that in this day and age, a successful general is hard to stop. I'm going to be serving on a governor's staff in Asia; I hope there's some fighting and I can get some military experience.

I know it's a while ago, but I wanted to offer my condolences on your brother's death. As you know, I don't have any brothers, but my sister Julia is alive and well and married to a man named Marcus Atius Balbus. He's from a distinguished family, unfortunately related to Pompey on his mother's side, but I guess Pompey's going to be a powerful man in the future, so maybe being related to him isn't all bad.

Written in 78 BC. It seems like you monarchical countries are always having civil wars when the old king dies. Then again, even though we're a republic, we may be heading for another civil war ourselves. In my last letter, I told you that Sulla had died, and that consequently I was headed back to Rome. When I got here, I found that one of the consuls, Marcus Aemilius Lepidus, was trying to re-enact a lot of the good old pre-Sulla legislation. He restored the subsidized grain program, he's promising to give back the land that Sulla took from the Italians, and there are even rumors that he wants to restore the full powers of the tribunes. But I don't know whether he's sincere or is just an opportunist looking for support from everyone that Sulla persecuted. I do know that I don't think too highly of his judgment, and if he's hoping for my support he can think again. I'm no Sullan, but we might as well work within the system as risk our lives trying to overthrow it.

I'd advise you to be cautious also. If the younger son looks much weaker than the older, then don't join him, regardless of whether you like him better. You won't be able to reform the government if you're dead.

Written in 77 BC. My advice is to lie low for a while. And bribe the right people. The king can't hold a grudge forever against everyone who supported his brother.

I'm lying low myself. Lepidus ended up in open rebellion against the Senate, but the other consul crushed him, with a lot of help from Pompey. A lot of Lepidus' supporters went to join Sertorius in Spain, so Pompey demanded that the Senate let him chase after them. I don't think all the senators were that sad to see him go: Pompey's a lot better soldier than Lepidus, and he's young and ambitious. Not exactly the kind of guy that the old timers in the Senate want to let get too powerful.

The old timers in the Senate aren't that fond of me, either, so I figured I'd better leave Rome again for a while until things settle down again. I'm on my way to the east to study oratory—all the top public speakers in Rome study oratory in the Greek east. I hope we don't run into pirates on the way. There are a lot of pirates in the Mediterranean these days. We really ought to do something to suppress them someday.

Written in 72 BC. I'm glad to hear you're back in favor again. When I went several years without hearing from you, I thought maybe you'd been executed.

Things are really in a mess around here. We're at war with Mithridates again; one of Sulla's old lieutenants is out in the east making only slow progress. Meanwhile, Pompey still hasn't defeated Sertorius, although he's had some success, and I think Sertorius' followers are getting disaffected. Back home, though, there's a slave revolt underway! We had slave revolts in Sicily some decades back, but this one is in Italy itself. Its leader is an escaped gladiator named Spartacus: he's organized his followers into an army and just defeated a force led by both consuls! So the Senate has appointed Crassus, another one of Sulla's old lieutenants, to command eight legions and crush the uprising before it destroys us. No one trusts Crassus, because he's rich and unscrupulous, but he's got some military talent. He might be a good man to have as a friend.

Anyway, it's pretty clear that Sulla's system isn't getting the job done. I think we need some revision, to let talented younger men have more say in affairs, instead of having the incompetent old nobles run everything.

I hope that the epidemic you mentioned is a short-run affair. Take care, and write back when you can.

This is the last letter; apparently Caesar's unknown correspondent died in the epidemic.

The History of Rome

Chapter Four

*in which the map turns sideways, but the rest of the chapter doesn't,
although the rest of the chapter is not without its stylistic oddities*

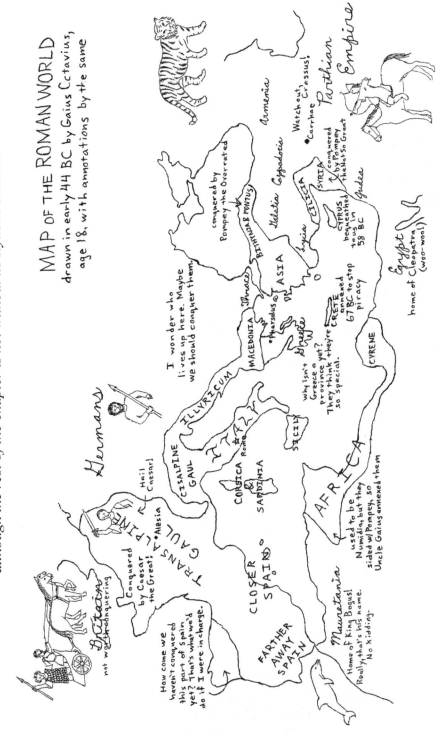

MAP OF THE ROMAN WORLD
drawn in early 44 BC by Gaius Octavius,
age 18, with annotations by the same

Germans

Hail
Caesar!

Britain
not worth conquering

Conquered
by Caesar
the Great!

• Alesia

TRANSALPINE
GAUL

CISALPINE
GAUL

How come we
haven't conquered
this part of Spain
yet? That's what we'd
do if I were in charge.

CLOSER
SPAIN

FARTHER
AWAY
SPAIN

Mauretania
Home of King Bogus!
Really, that's his name.
No kidding.

CORSICA
&
SARDINIA

ITALY
★ Rome

SICILY

AFRICA

used to be
Numidia, but they
sided w/ Pompey, so
Uncle Gaius annexed them

ILLYRICUM

MACEDONIA

Thrace

• Pharsalus

Epirus

Achaea

I wonder who
lives up here. Maybe
we should conquer them.

why isn't
Greece a
province yet?
They think they're
so special.

CRETE
annexed
67 BC to stop
piracy

CYRENE

conquered by
Pompey the Overrated

BITHYNIA & PONTUS

Galatia Cappadocia

ASIA

Lycia

CILICIA

Armenia

Watch out,
• Carrhae Crassus!

Parthian
Empire

SYRIA

conquered
by Pompey
the No So Great

CYPRUS
bequeathed
to us in
58 BC

Judea

Egypt
home of Cleopatra
(woo-woo!)

We Can Work it Out, We Can Work it Out

One day in 71 BC, Crassus and Pompey were sitting around outside Rome with their armies.

"Okay, Pompey," said Crassus, "let's cut to the chase. You don't like me and I don't like you."

"You're just jealous because Sulla always liked me better," said Pompey.

"Forget Sulla. We've got a problem. You defeated the Spanish rebels, I crushed the slave revolt—"

"With some help from me."

"You just mopped up the fugitives after I'd destroyed Spartacus' army. I remind you that you couldn't even win in Spain until Sertorius was assassinated by a disgruntled subordinate."

"Yeah? Which one of us do the Roman people like better? I've never heard of anyone calling you Crassus the Great."

"Look, we could trade insults all day. The point is, we both want to be consul, but the Senate doesn't like us and will stop us if they can."

"I'm way ahead of you. We've got armies, the Senate doesn't."

"Exactly. They're hoping to play us off against each other, but if we join forces, they'll be intimidated into letting us be elected."

"The problem, though, is that under Sulla's constitution, the Senate will have the upper hand again as soon as our term is over."

"So we'll change the constitution. Restore the censorship. I'd make a good censor."

> **I am Spartacus!**
>
> Okay, actually, I'm not. But that's what all of the captured slaves said at the end of the movie *Spartacus*, when Crassus said they could live if Spartacus would identify himself so the Romans could crucify him. It was a stirring scene. In the end, Crassus just crucified all six thousand of them instead.
>
> In the early 1900's, a couple of German communists organized a Spartacus League to try to start a revolution. They failed and were executed without a trial. Maybe they should have chosen a more successful namesake.

"Yeah, so you can pack the Senate with people who owe you money. We also need to restore the full powers of the tribunate."

"So you can use your popularity with the urban rabble to pass laws giving you special powers? Okay, so long as I get to give the equites some political influence again."

Portrait of Pompey
as a Young Man

"Always looking out for your businessmen buddies, huh? Fine, they'll help keep the old senatorial fogies in line. By the way, we should also pardon all of Lepidus' old followers who are still hiding out in exile. They'll all support the new order."

"Yeah, I already thought of that myself. So it's agreed? Joint consulship for us, we get land grants for our veterans, and undo all of Sulla's constitutional changes?"

"Agreed. Of course you realize I'm still far more influential and important than you are.

"In your dreams, fat boy, in your dreams."

The Roman Daily News

Mithridatic War Drags On and On
by Q. Marcius Rex

ASIA MINOR (67 BC)-- The recent announcement that the Roman people have lost confidence in L. Licinius Lucullus, Roman commander in Asia, has done little to bolster the fortunes of Roman arms in the struggle against Mithridates. The wily Pontic ruler, earlier defeats notwithstanding, has returned to his kingdom while Lucullus is hamstrung by disaffection among his troops and officers. The nomination of the consul Glabrio as Lucullus' replacement has failed to boost morale, since, while Lucullus' strict discipline alienated his men, he is at least regarded as a better general than Glabrio. Threats of intervention by the Parthian Empire have also disheartened Rome's armies. Meanwhile, the people of the provinces of Asia, Cilicia, and *(see **Mithridatic War**--p. Avi)*

Gabinius Nominates Pompey for Command against Pirates
by M. Terentius Varro

ROME (67 BC)--Tribune Aulus Gabinius has nominated ex-consul Pompey the Great for a special command against the pirates who have been plaguing the Mediterranean for decades now. Wealthy Romans who fall into the hands of these sea-raiders are held for ransom; their poorer compatriots are sold into slavery. The government's failure to suppress the pirates has lost the Senate credit with the people, and has lost Rome credit with her allies overseas.

The proposal in question would grant Pompey extraordinary authority to raise troops, build fleets, and give orders to commanders of Roman provinces. Gabinius charges that Rome's previous efforts to defeat the pirates have been hampered by the division of authority among several different regional commanders, along with the general incompetence of the men appointed by the Senate.

Given Pompey's popularity with the people of Rome, and the fact that Gabinius intends to take his proposal directly to the popular assembly without seeking approval from the Senate, it seems certain that the proposal will pass. Whether Pompey will succeed where others before him have failed is, however, much less certain. Although Pompey has considerable experience as a *(see **Pompey**--p. Aix)*

News Analysis
Senate's Influence on the Wane
by L. Calpurnius

The expected passage of the proposal giving extraordinary power to Pompey the Great will confirm what conservative senators have feared ever since the consulship of Crassus and Pompey three years ago: with Sulla's constitution undone, the authority of the Senate is but a small counterweight to the ambitions of popular generals, especially when the latter can win the support of the majority of the equites. In the present instance, support from the *(see **Senate**--p. Aix)*

Inside Today's Issue

Business: Crassus Tops List of Rome's Wealthiest Men
Society: Widower Caesar Marries Sulla's Granddaughter
Sports: Greek Charioteer Empedocles Wins Third Victory in a Row

Corruption in Provinces Unabated
by M. Atilius Regulus

AFRICA (67 BC)--Despite numerous recent prosecutions, notably the conviction of former Sicilian governor C. Verres engineered by new man, outstanding orator, and rising politician M. Tullius Cicero, provincial governors continue to be both corrupt and tyrannical. In Africa, the dissolute patrician L. Sergius Catilina became governor this year *(see **Corruption**--p. Aiv)*

A Diagram is Worth 719 Words

Pompey defeated the pirates in just three months, which was much faster than he or anyone else had expected and left him with nothing to do. Luckily, the war against Mithridates was still dragging on, so a tribune proposed giving the command to Pompey. The conservative leaders of the Senate, the so-called Optimates, opposed the proposal, but both Caesar and the orator Marcus Tullius Cicero favored it. They thought that Rome's failure to crush Mithridates was disgraceful; at the same time, they thought that it wouldn't hurt their political careers to be on Pompey's good side. The people voted for the proposal, of course, and Pompey went off to the east.

Crassus was worried by Pompey's ever-increasing prestige, so he spent the next few years trying to increase his own influence, especially by giving political and financial support to other politicians, including during his censorship in 65 BC. Cicero stood up for Pompey's interests by opposing Crassus' maneuvers, while Caesar managed to remain friendly with Pompey and Crassus simultaneously. Meanwhile, the Optimates were suspicious of all of these prominent men whose popularity with the voters threatened the Senate's predominance.

In 64 BC, Cicero ran for the consulship. Crassus and Caesar backed his opponent Catiline, a noble who tried to win popularity through radical proposals on behalf of debtors and other unhappy proletarians. Catiline's campaign promises backfired by causing the Optimates to support Cicero, who was elected by a wide margin. During the year 63, while Cicero was consul, Catiline ran for the consulship again, though this time without Crassus' support; Crassus, who was Rome's biggest creditor, had apparently decided that Catiline was serious about debt cancellation. Catiline lost again and decided to hell with elections, he was going to have a revolution. A bunch of other dissolute noblemen joined in his conspiracy, but Cicero found out about it and denounced Catiline in the Senate. Catiline fled to the countryside, where some of his co-conspirators were trying to raise an army from the rural proletarians. Cicero summarily executed some conspirators who'd been caught in the city, brushing aside the protests of Caesar, who was suspected of secretly supporting Catiline even now. After the executions, most of the motley revolutionary army deserted, and Catiline was killed in battle. The Optimates, who'd always looked down on Cicero as a new man, decided that maybe he wasn't so bad after all.

> ### More About Cicero
>
> Cicero is one of the most famous ancient Romans: a brilliant orator, a masterful writer of Latin prose, and a skillful politician who fought long and hard to preserve the senatorial dominance which he believed to be the foundation of Roman glory. We know a great deal about his character because many hundreds of his private letters survive to this day. He was honest in an age when almost all Roman politicians were corrupt, a faithful husband at a time when wealthy Romans of both sexes were notoriously faithless. Witty, inordinately vain, admired by younger contemporaries like Caesar, eventually viewed by many as an old-fashioned idealist out of touch with his times, Cicero remains one of the Rome's most fascinating personalities.
>
> There's a city named after Cicero in Illinois, just west of Chicago. It's famous for serving as Al Capone's headquarters in the early 20th century.

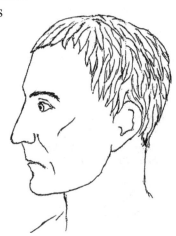

Caesar is Shocked, Shocked, to be Suspected of Complicity with Catiline

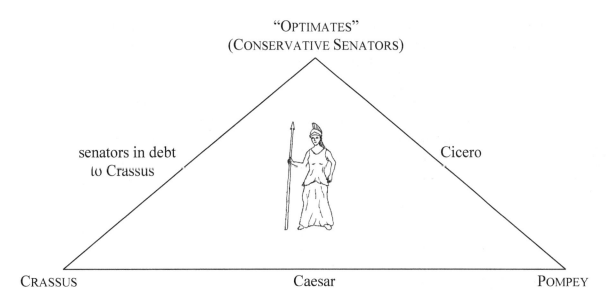

"OPTIMATES"
(CONSERVATIVE SENATORS)

senators in debt
to Crassus

Cicero

CRASSUS

Caesar

POMPEY

THE ROMAN POWER TRIANGLE IN THE 60's BC

For the rest of his life, Cicero was convinced that he had saved Rome from disaster and thus was the Republic's greatest living statesman. Unfortunately, the glory of his achievement was somewhat overshadowed by the imminent return of Pompey. Pompey had not only defeated Mithridates and annexed his kingdom, he had also annexed Syria and established friendly relations with other eastern powers. Now he was on his way back to Rome with his army, and everyone was worried lest he imitate Sulla and use his army to make himself dictator. But Pompey saw no reason why he should overthrow a system in which he was doing so well. Instead, he disbanded his army and waited for the Senate to ratify his settlement of the east while providing land for his veterans.

Surprise! The Senate refused to do either. Crassus undoubtedly had a hand in frustrating his rival, but soon Crassus developed problems of his own when his friends among the equites overbid for government contracts and then couldn't get the Senate to give them a rebate. Once again, the Optimates were playing Crassus and Pompey off against one another.

That's how matters stood when Caesar, who had been off governing Farther Away Spain, returned to Rome in 60 BC to stand for the consulship. Being on friendly terms with both Crassus and Pompey, he struck a deal whereby they would support his candidacy, and once in office, he would use any means necessary to advance their interests; historians now normally refer to this grouping of three men as the First Triumvirate. With Crassus and Pompey both backing Caesar, the Optimates were powerless to keep him out of office. However, through massive use of bribery, they did manage to bring about the election of an Optimate with the unlikely name of Bibulus as Caesar's colleague, in hopes of frustrating Caesar's agenda. Thus, the stage was set for the consulship of Bibulus and Caesar.

The Consulship of Julius and Caesar

Caesar, it turned out, was not very keen on having his agenda frustrated. So he arranged for hired thugs to assault Bibulus when the latter left his house to take part in public business. Bibulus eventually gave up leaving his house, and witty Romans started calling the year 59 the consulship of Julius and Caesar.

Meanwhile, Caesar's attempts to win over Cicero, now a leader of the Optimates, were unavailing, and it became clear that the Senate wasn't going to support any of Caesar's proposals. So he took them to the popular assemblies instead. Supported, again, by bands of thugs, as well as by some ambitious tribunes, he soon got a rebate for Crassus' friends, land for Pompey's veterans, ratification of Pompey's eastern settlement, and, for himself, a five-year governorship in Illyricum and Cisalpine Gaul, to which Transalpine Gaul was later added. To keep Crassus friendly, Caesar agreed to bring Crassus' son with him to the provinces as one of his lieutenants. He also arranged a couple of marriage alliances: Caesar's daughter Julia married Pompey, and Caesar himself, having divorced his second wife in 62, married a noble's daughter and then got his new father-in-law elected consul for 58.

Having arranged things in Rome to suit the Triumvirate, Caesar went off to Cisalpine Gaul to raise an army. The army could be used in the future for two purposes: to intimidate the Triumvirate's enemies in Rome, and to conquer some foreign peoples so that Caesar could get enough plunder to pay off his debts, which were considerable. Election campaigns weren't cheap in those days, let alone the cost of hired thugs.

A Happy Marriage

Excerpts from the diary of Caesar's only legitimate child, Julia, his daughter by his first wife, Cornelia. Modern historians believe that Julia was a teenager when she married Pompey.

Written in early 59 BC
I am going to marry Gnaeus Pompeius! The most illustrious man in Rome! Of course I know it's all about politics, but still, I'll be mistress of one of the finest households in Rome. I guess he's a little bit older than I'd like, but he's not bad-looking in a distinguished sort of way. And he's a very respectable man, not like these wild young aristocrats. Like Publius Clodius. Ugh! I'd rather be a Vestal Virgin than marry someone like him. And Pompey's very nice. Not a witty conversationalist like Daddy or Cicero, but dignified and polite. I think he likes me, too.

Written in the middle of 59 BC
What a wonderful husband I have! So affectionate!

Written in late 59 BC
It's amazing what vicious gossip you can hear in Rome. People are saying that Gnaeus is embarrassed by the tactics Daddy has been using. I asked Gnaeus about it, and he said that he and Daddy are still friends. He said that if the senators weren't so pigheaded Daddy wouldn't have to resort to those kinds of tactics.

Written in early 58 BC
I haven't had a letter from Daddy for a while. I've heard that he took his army into northern Gaul to help out some of our allies. I hope he's careful and doesn't get himself hurt. I'm glad that Gnaeus is spending his time at home instead of campaigning. I'd get so lonely without him.

Clodius, who's a tribune now, is trying to get Cicero exiled because he executed those conspirators without giving them a trial. Poor Cicero! Apparently Clodius has some personal grudge against him. Gnaeus says he feels bad for Cicero, but there's nothing he can do about it.

Written in late 58 BC

Gnaeus gave me the most wonderful present today! An emerald necklace all the way from Syria! My cousin Atia, Aunt Julia's daughter, was visiting, and she was really jealous. Her little son Gaius came with her. He's so cute! He must be about five years old now.

Written in early 57 BC

Something has to be done about that Clodius. It wasn't enough for him to get Cicero exiled, now he's put together gangs of hooligans who rampage around the streets and have even threatened Gnaeus! Gnaeus says he thinks Crassus is behind the whole thing. Someone has to pay the hooligans, after all. But a brave tribune named Milo has put together bands of volunteers to defend law and order against those criminals. I'm still worried, though. Crassus and Clodius are dangerous men, and Gnaeus is so brave that he might not be careful enough.

I wish Daddy could come home, but apparently some of the Gauls attacked him, and he's having to defend Rome's interests. That's what he said in his last letter, anyway.

Written in late 57 BC

Cicero returned to the city today, and everyone (except Clodius) was so happy to see him. Everybody is complimenting Gnaeus on taking the lead in getting Cicero recalled. Now I'm sure that Cicero will be friendly with Gnaeus in the future.

Written in early 56 BC

I can't believe all this talk about a rift between Daddy and Gnaeus. To think that people would accuse Daddy of supporting Clodius! Even Crassus seems to be distancing himself from Clodius. Poor Gnaeus. I think he'd really like to retire and just enjoy life, but he's got too much of a sense of duty. As long as Daddy is away, someone in Rome has to stand up for what's right. Anyway, Gnaeus says he's going to go meet with Daddy and Crassus in some town in northern Italy and try to hash out an agreement that will be good for everyone. Probably Daddy will have his command extended, and Gnaeus and Crassus will get to be consuls next year.

Atia says that everyone in Italy is excited about Daddy's successes in Gaul. It's so nice that he's getting a military reputation to equal Gnaeus'. Gnaeus is actually a little jealous of Daddy now, which is kind of cute. Men have such fragile egos.

Written in early 55 BC

Gnaeus says that he's not going to Spain next year after all. He'll still be assigned the governorship of both provinces, but he can send out lieutenants to run them for him. Good news! I'd get lonely with him gone for five years. Crassus is still going in person to Syria, though. Apparently he's jealous of Gnaeus and Daddy and wants to become a successful general himself. I don't think there'll be anyone for him to fight, though, since Gnaeus did such a good job of settling the east when he was there.

Written in early 54 BC

Daddy may think that his invasion of Britain is big news, but I have even bigger news for him—I'm pregnant! Gnaeus is delighted.

Julia died in childbirth in 54 BC; her newborn child died a few days later.

Civil War

After Julia's death, events moved quickly. Caesar found out that Britain was harder to conquer than he'd expected, so he gave up and went back to Gaul at the end of 54 BC. He spent the next couple of years suppressing revolts among the Gauls, who, when they had invited Caesar to come and help them fight their enemies, had not expected him to stay and conquer all of Gaul himself. Silly Gauls.

Crassus, meanwhile, accompanied by the son who had previously fought under Caesar, went to Syria and decided to launch an invasion of the Parthian Empire. He didn't have much of a pretext for doing so, but Caesar hadn't had much of a pretext for conquering Gaul, either, and he'd still become enormously rich and popular through his conquests. However, the Parthians turned out to be a formidable foe. At the battle of Carrhae in 53 BC, they destroyed Crassus' army of three legions, and both Crassus and his son were killed.

Meanwhile, back at Rome, Clodius and Milo were continuing to cause havoc with their gangs of roughnecks. Both men hoped to rise to the consulship someday, Clodius by winning the support of the urban poor, Milo by winning the backing of influential men like Pompey and Cicero. The street battles that they engaged in prevented the elections for 52 from being held. Early in 52, though, Clodius and Milo, accompanied by some of their henchmen, bumped into each other on a road outside of Rome. A fracas ensued, Clodius' men were bested, and Clodius was killed at Milo's orders.

Clodius' supporters in the city were so outraged by his murder that they rioted and burned down the Senate house. Plainly, a dictator was needed to restore order, and Pompey was the obvious choice. The Senate, remembering Sulla's proscriptions, decided to designate Pompey sole consul instead of dictator, but it amounted to the same thing. Pompey brought soldiers into the city, restored order, and saw to it that Milo was convicted of murder and sent into exile.

Caesar spent the year 52 restoring order in Gaul, where a fellow named Vercingetorix was leading a major revolt. Caesar eventually captured Vercingetorix at a town named Alesia, but the French still think of Vercingetorix as their first national hero. There's a big statue of him at Alesia today.

Thus Pompey became master in Rome while Caesar became master in Gaul. The Optimates decided they could work with Pompey. Caesar, on the other hand, they saw as the heir of Marius, Cinna, Lepidus, and Catiline: men who employed demagoguery and military force in their efforts to overthrow the rule of the Senate. Pompey himself dithered for the next couple of years. He liked being the de facto ruler of Rome, supported by the Senate and by troops in both Italy and the provinces. But he wasn't sure he wanted to break his old alliance with Caesar. Eventually, leading Optimates like Cato the Younger, great-grandson of Cato the Censor, brought matters to a head by plotting to remove Caesar from his command and prosecute him for his various unconstitutional acts, including his unauthorized conquest of Gaul. In late 50 BC, Pompey finally decided to support the Optimate plan. When Caesar refused to lay down his command unless Pompey did likewise, the Senate declared Caesar an outlaw and authorized Pompey to take any steps necessary to save the state.

Portrait of Pompey
as an Older Man

Caesar, Just after Hearing that He's Been Outlawed

It was winter, and all but one of Caesar's legions were north of the Alps. Pompey had only a few troops in Italy, but plenty in Spain, so he planned on spending the early part of 49 raising more troops in Italy. Then, in spring, he could march his Italian troops into Cisalpine Gaul and his Spanish ones into Transalpine Gaul.

Caesar, however, was not a dummy, and he knew that delay would work to Pompey's advantage. So he marched into Italy with his one Cisalpine legion, and most of Pompey's raw recruits ran away rather than face Caesar's veterans. It turned out that most of the people of Italy had no interest in fighting to support Pompey and the Optimates, so that within two months, Pompey and his supporters had to abandon Italy and go to Macedonia to try to regroup.

While Pompey spent the whole year building up an army in Macedonia, Caesar took most of his army to Spain and defeated Pompey's lieutenants there. Then, knowing as always that delay would just give Pompey time to raise more troops, he sailed from Italy to Macedonia in the winter, an unexpected move given that it was dangerous to sail in the winter in the unseaworthy craft of those days. Several months of campaigning followed: Pompey had a larger army and more cavalry, but Caesar's battle-tested infantry were superior in quality to Pompey's recruits. In early June of 48 BC, at a site called Pharsalus in northern Greece, Caesar's army destroyed Pompey's and sent its generals fleeing to the four winds.

Pompey himself fled to Egypt, where the king, who was scared that Caesar would get upset if Pompey were given refuge, had the unfortunate general murdered. Caesar showed up in Egypt himself soon thereafter and got involved in local politics, mostly because he got personally involved with the king's sister and co-ruler, Cleopatra. Cleopatra, talented and ambitious, didn't care for sharing power with her feckless younger brother, and she reasoned that with Caesar's help she could shove her brother out of the way entirely. Caesar obliged—Cleopatra, though not especially beautiful, was young and possessed legendary charm, while Caesar had always been notoriously fond of extramarital affairs.

Dalliance with a queen of the east is a lot of fun, presumably, but eventually Caesar realized that he should probably go finish off those of his enemies who had gathered in Africa and Spain, where they had raised new armies. In between doing so, he spent some time at Rome, where he reorganized the government, gave land to his veterans, established colonies, created a new and more accurate calendar, and generally passed a whole lot of worthwhile legislation. The equites, the urban poor, the people of Italy, pretty much everyone except the Senate saw how efficient a dictatorial regime could be in addressing Rome's social and economic problems.

By 45 BC, the last of the Pompeians were defeated, and Caesar found himself undisputed master of the Roman world. Never a vindictive sort, and eager to put an end to civil strife, he let most of his former Optimate enemies (e.g., Cicero) come back to Rome as senators, although Cato committed suicide and Pompey's only surviving son remained at large. Being a senator wasn't as much fun as it had been, though, since Caesar had himself named dictator for life and obviously had no interest in restoring the Senate to its former dominant position.

Discontented senators notwithstanding, many people were happy with the new regime. At least the civil wars were over, and the Roman world could look forward to decades of uninterrupted peace and prosperity at home, along with glorious wars of conquest overseas. Or so it seemed on the morning of March 15, 44 BC.

The End of the Republic

Dramatis Personae: Prof. Fusterman and a couple dozen rather bored students.

Cicero is Discontented

Fusterman: It is, ah, commonly held that the Republic died in the year 27 BC. That, of course, is poppycock. The Republic's death was long and drawn out, but if we are to name any date for its final demise, the year 42 would be most appropriate.

Student #1 (to Student #2, whispering): Does he mean BC or AD?

Fusterman: For it was in that year that the Senate's armies met their final defeat, at, ah, what battle, Miss, ah, Heligan?

Student #3 (sleepily): Umm...what?

Fusterman: Quite. Mr. Hashimoto?

Student #2 (hurriedly paging through his textbook): Umm...Philippi?

Fusterman: The usual English pronunciation, Mr. Hashimoto, is Philipp-eye, not Philipp-ee. But as the ancients pronounced it as -ee, I suppose you may be forgiven. Now, Miss Wysocki, who were the leaders of the senatorial army?

Student #4: Umm, was that Brutus and Cassius?

Fusterman: Indeed. Seeing as you seem to have done the reading, Miss Wysocki, perhaps you would be so good as to summarize it for your classmates.

Student #4 (who has not actually done the reading, but who saw a movie version of Shakespeare's play Julius Caesar *in high school English class):* Umm...okay. Umm, so Caesar wanted to be king, or something, but the Senate didn't want him to be, so Brutus and Cassius and some other senators assassinated him—

Fusterman: On what date, Miss Wysocki?

Student #4: Umm...the Ides of March?

Fusterman: Which is what day of the month?

Student #4: March 1st?

Fusterman: No. That would be the Calends, which word gives us the English word calendar. Mr. Denton?

Student #5 (bored, and very sure of himself): March 15th. Beware the Ides of March.

Fusterman: Sage advice, Mr. Denton. Please continue, Miss Wysocki.

Student #4: Okay. So but then Mark Antony stirred up the crowd, and the people turned on the assassins, and then Octavius came and he and Mark Antony took over and fought the conspirators and killed them. At the battle of Philippi.

Fusterman: Very good, Miss Wysocki. Mr. Kelly. You seemed amused by the mention of Mark Antony.

Student #6: Oh, sorry. I, like, didn't do the reading. I thought she was joking.

Fusterman: Is there something humorous about Mark Antony?

Student #6: There's this pop singer named Marc Anthony. He's really famous.

Fusterman: No doubt. So was the general Marcus Antonius in his day. A former tribune, he fought for Caesar in both the Gallic and the Civil Wars and was Caesar's co-consul in the year 44 BC. The conspirators considered killing him as well but decided not to, to their regret, since, as Miss Wysocki tells us, he stirred up the urban rabble against the assassins, causing them to flee to the eastern provinces, where they raised troops for the inevitable civil war.

Student #1 (to Student #2, whispering): Didn't Shakespeare write a play about Antony and Cleopatra?

Student #7 (muttering as he feverishly scrawls in his notebook): ...inevitable civil war...

Student #8 (raising her hand): I have a question about Octavius. The book said that he was called Octavian after 44 BC, but it didn't say why.

Fusterman (writing both names on the blackboard): Gaius Octavius was Caesar's grandnephew, the grandson of Caesar's sister Julia. Since Caesar had no children of his own, his daughter Julia having died, he adopted Octavius in his will. On hearing of the adoption, Octavius, who was only eighteen at the time and was studying in Macedonia, hurried back to Rome to claim his inheritance. As Caesar's adoptive son, he became known as Gaius Julius Caesar Octavianus, from the last of which names we derive the English name Octavian.

Student #8: I was also wondering about Brutus. Was he related to the guy that threw out, um, what was his name, Tarquinius Priscus?

Fusterman: Tarquinius Superbus, actually, the son or grandson of Tarquinius Priscus. But yes, Marcus Junius Brutus was a descendant of that Lucius Junius Brutus who overthrew the monarchy. He thus felt a particular, ah, familial obligation to overthrow Caesar's autocratic rule. Both Brutus and Cassius, by the way, fought for Pompey but were pardoned by Caesar.

Student #7 (muttering): ...Brutus fought for Popeye...

Student #2: What about Cicero? Was he in on the assassination?

Fusterman: Mr. Garcia? Any thoughts?

Student #9: Well, I guess so, because didn't Antony have him killed? I think they chopped off his head and hands and put them on display in the Forum.

Student #3 (startled into wakefulness): Eww, really?

Fusterman: They did indeed, Miss Heligan. After Caesar's murder, there was a rather confused period in which the Senate, along with various of Caesar's officers, competed for power. Cicero, who was, ah, delighted by the assassination, did his utmost to unite all parties against Antony, whom he saw as another would-be dictator. But when young Octavian, who had at first sided with Cicero, later joined with Antony instead, the Senate had no army with which to oppose the reunited Caesarian party. Octavian, Antony, and another Caesarian named Lepidus formed the Second Triumvirate, took the city of Rome, and proscribed thousands of their opponents.

Student #10: You mean like Sulla did? They killed them?

Fusterman: Exactly. And for the same reasons, to quell the opposition and to confiscate their property, which they needed for the support of their troops.

Student #7 (muttering): ...Sulla prescribed Triumvirate...

Fusterman: Naturally, Antony had Cicero killed.

Student #5 (with a tone of condescension): But, to answer John's question, no, Cicero wasn't in on the assassination attempt.

Fusterman: Quite right, quite right, Mr. Denton. Though he was, ah, delighted at its outcome, as I indicated. The point being, ah, that the assassination of Caesar was the last-ditch effort of the die-hard senatorial faction to maintain their oligarchic rule. A quixotic endeavor, to be sure. Soldiers and average citizens alike preferred the efficient rule of a dictator to that of the corrupt, selfish, and narrow-minded aristocracy. The Senate had ruled by virtue of its moral authority. Once it lost the respect of the people and the army, the latter withdrew their support, and the entire rotten edifice collapsed.

Student #1 (to Student #2, whispering): What? What did he say about Oedipus?

Student #8: Wow. So, like, if Brutus and Cassius had won that battle, wouldn't they have restored the Republic?

Fusterman: Brutus and Cassius themselves raised armies on their own authority. Of course, they claimed to do so in the name of the Senate, but the Triumvirs claimed likewise. To be certain, Brutus and Cassius might have tried to imitate Marius and put the Senate back in authority—

Student #5: Sulla.

Fusterman: Of course, of course, to imitate not Marius, but Sulla, and, ah, restore the authority of the Senate. But in an age when generals could raise personal armies at their whim, such an effort would have collapsed more rapidly even than Sulla's constitution had done. At any rate, the conspirators did lose the battle of Philippi in 42 BC, leaving the state completely under the control of Caesar's successors. And the Roman Republic was dead. Which, ah, brings this chapter to a close.

Final Exam Grades History 214	
Student #1	72
Student #2	83
Student #3	64
Student #4	80
Student #5	99
Student #6	68
Student #7	56
Student #8	91
Student #9	90
Student #10	87
Student #11	76
Student #12	88
Student #13	85

Student #11 (to student #5, whispering): But didn't they restore the Republic after Maximus killed Commodus?

Student #12 (sotto voce): You watch too many movies.

Hail, Caesar!

Julius Caesar is the most famous Roman of them all. The month July was named after him, and the name Caesar is preserved in such important terms as Kaiser, Czar, and Caesar salad. After his death, the Caesarian faction got the Senate to vote that Caesar had become a god, which allowed Octavian, thereafter, to call himself the son of a god, a valuable bit of propaganda. All of which suggests that maybe we should say a little bit more about old Gaius Julius before moving to his successors in the next chapter.

Caesar was not just a talented general and politician, he was also an orator second only to Cicero in his day, and a writer of clear and compelling Latin prose. His governmental reforms during his dictatorship were far-reaching and far-sighted. He aimed to rein in governmental corruption; help out debtors, the Roman poor, and oppressed provincials; and bring stability and internal peace to the Roman world. His opponents feared that he would lead a social revolution, cancelling all debts, expropriating the estates of the wealthy, and giving the proceeds to the proletarians. The radicalism of his early career gave credence to these fears, but as dictator he surprised everyone by his moderation. His assassination was motivated not so much by the nature of his reforms as by his unapologetically dictatorial methods of enacting them, along his unhidden disdain for the old constitution.

On a personal level, Caesar is said to have possessed great charm. Quick-witted and an engaging conversationalist, he was quite the bon vivant as a young man. Vain and very careful about his appearance, he was exceedingly popular with the ladies, including other men's wives, with whom he had numerous affairs throughout his life. His political enemies alleged that he had also had a youthful liaison with the king of Bithynia; though unprovable at this date, the claim was widely believed in Caesar's day. Like most scions of the nobility in the late Republic, Caesar was profligate with borrowed money, getting so far into debt that only the plundering of a province could return him to solvency. In the event, his conquest and despoliation of Gaul made him immensely rich, and he used his wealth to buy the loyalty of his soldiers and the support of other politicians.

A final question is, what did he look like? There are numerous surviving sculptural depictions of Caesar. Although they're all recognizably images of the same person, they often differ substantially as to specific physical features. Presumably, many sculptors idealized their powerful subject, making him handsomer than he was in real life. Nevertheless, there are some commonalities: a long bony face, hollow cheeks, close-set eyes, prominent Roman nose, wide mouth, pointy chin, long skinny neck, and (interestingly enough) long earlobes. Also, as he aged, his hairline receded ever further: our written sources tell us that he was very happy when, as dictator, he was allowed to cover his baldness with a laurel wreath. Commonalities notwithstanding, I found it very hard to draw Caesar; the drawings in this chapter are the best I could manage, after several less satisfactory efforts. For your amusement, I've included here an earlier attempt, to which I added sunglasses after I decided that the eyes didn't look right. You can think of it as a picture of Caesar reincarnated as an Italian movie producer.

Speaking of portraits, I should mention that the pictures of Marius, Sulla, Pompey, and Cicero are also all based on actual ancient sculptural depictions. There are numerous sculptures of leading Romans from the late Republic onward, though not of everyone (plus, some sculptures might or might not really be portraits of the people that they're commonly believed to depict). Most surviving Republic-era sculptures are portrait busts, and many of them are marvelous works of art, combining unflinching naturalism with keen psychological insight. However, the idealization seen in many depictions of Caesar also shows up in some other sculptures. For example, there are two particularly famous sculptures of Pompey, one a heroic portrait of a young conqueror, the other a less flattering and presumably more accurate depiction of Pompey as an older man. They hardly even look like the same person, so my picture of young Pompey, though based on that idealized sculpture, is modified somewhat so that he looks a little more like his older self and a little less like SuperRoman.

If you don't like my pictures of Caesar, feel free to draw your own and paste them over the ones in this book. Likewise for Marius, Sulla, Pompey, Cicero, and all the people in future chapters. I won't be offended.

Study Questions for Chapter Four

1. When did the Roman Republic fall?
   - (a) 59 BC
   - (b) 42 BC
   - (c) 27 BC
   - (d) October 8 at 3:17 pm

2. Why did the Roman Republic fall?
   - (a) unscrupulous politicians
   - (b) narrow-minded Optimates
   - (c) land-hungry soldiers
   - (d) giant space rats

3. How did the Roman Republic fall?
   - (a) quickly and unexpectedly, like a quarterback blindsided by a blitzing linebacker
   - (b) slowly and painfully, like a moose savaged by a pack of wolves
   - (c) loudly and complainingly, like a fat man sliding off the roof of his house
   - (d) sadly and statefully, like a mighty oak felled by the woodsman's axe

4. Have *you* ever tried to draw a picture of Caesar? Why or why not?

Psychiatric Interlude

THERAPIST: So, Mr. Lepidus, I believe when we left off last time, we were discussing your feelings of inadequacy?

LEPIDUS: What feelings of inadequacy? I'm not inadequate. I'm a triumvir, just like Antony and Octavian.

THERAPIST: *(making a note of the fact that Lepidus said "triumvir" with a lower-case "t")* And yet, since their victory at Philippi, they have treated you as a junior partner in all but name.

LEPIDUS: Exactly. It's not that I'm inadequate, it's just that everyone else treats me that way.

THERAPIST: I see. And how does that make you feel?

LEPIDUS: I don't want to talk about this. I don't even know what I'm paying you for.

THERAPIST: You may recall that you were having dreams that disturbed you considerably. Dreams involving your father—

LEPIDUS: All right, all right, I remember. So why don't you tell me what my dreams mean?

THERAPIST: Have you had any particularly disturbing dreams recently?

LEPIDUS: Just last night. I was standing in the Forum, and Caesar was standing next to me with his hand on my shoulder. "My right hand man," he said, only it was his left hand on my shoulder. I don't know what that means.

THERAPIST: *(glancing at his sundial)* Please continue.

LEPIDUS: So anyway, all of a sudden Caesar was dead, and I was looking around confused, and then Antony and Octavian and I were trying to get through a gate, but it was only wide enough for one person. Then Antony poked me in the eyeball, and Octavian shoved me into the dirt, and then they started fighting each other. I remember thinking it was sort of like a Three Stooges bit.

THERAPIST: I'm sorry. What's a Three Stooges bit?

LEPIDUS: I have no idea. It's just something I thought of in the dream

THERAPIST: Perhaps your dream was prophetic. So what happened next?

LEPIDUS: Then I was an old man, sitting around in some Italian town, drinking wine and waiting to die. And people kept walking by and saying, "Just like his father, just like his father."

THERAPIST: Your father being the failed revolutionary consul of 78 BC?

LEPIDUS: Yes. I told you all that last time.

THERAPIST: And did your father himself appear in this dream?

LEPIDUS: Yes, right at the end. He was a ghost, and he was bleeding from his death wounds, but he had a sort of happy smile on his face, and he said, "Second-rate isn't so bad, son. It's better than no rate at all." And I tried to shout out, "I'm not a second-rater! I'm not! I'm not!" but he reached out with his long bony hands and started choking the life out of me, and then I woke up in a cold sweat. I had to drink a whole bottle of cheap wine before I could get back to sleep again.

THERAPIST: You want my advice?

LEPIDUS: Why else am I here?

THERAPIST: Listen to your father. And stop drinking so much cheap wine.

THE HISTORY OF ROME

Chapter Five

*in which the Roman Republic turns into the Roman Empire, and most people are a lot better off,
apart from the people who get killed and maimed in imperial wars of conquest*

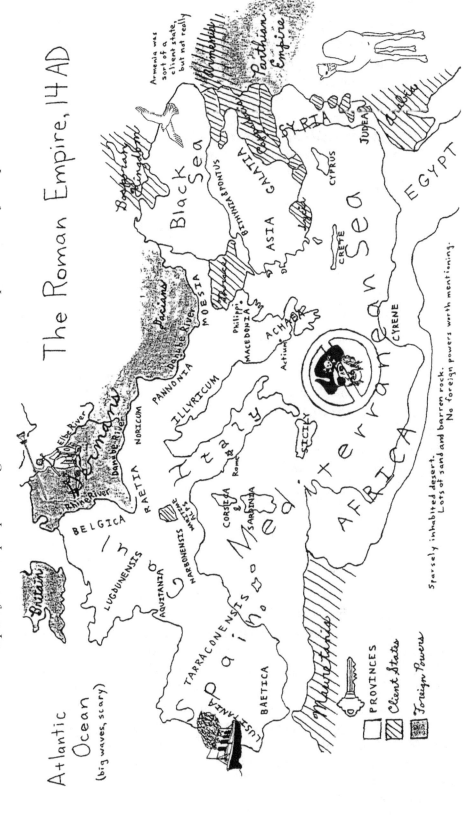

The Roman Empire, 14 AD

Atlantic Ocean
(big waves, scary)

Armenia was sort of a client state, but not really.

Parthian Empire

Sparsely inhabited desert.
Lots of sand and barren rock.
No foreign powers worth mentioning.

PROVINCES
Client States
Foreign Powers

Octavian vs. Antony (and Cleopatra)

Having killed Caesar's assassins and shoved Lepidus aside, Antony and Octavian were undisputed masters of the Roman world. They now had two options: *(1) They could lay down their special powers as Triumvirs and restore the full authority of the Senate and the popular assemblies. (2) They could keep power for themselves.*

Guess which option they chose.

Having chosen Option #2, the two potentates now had a further decision to make: *(1) They could divide the burdens of rulership equitably and work together to try to bring peace and prosperity to the entire Mediterranean. (2) They could each take a chunk of territory and then spend the next ten years trying to elbow the other guy off of the platform of power.*

The Platform of Power

Option #2 once again being the preferred choice, Antony, who was a good general, got to go to the east to win glory by fighting against the Parthians, who'd been causing problems ever since they whupped up on Crassus. Octavian, who was a lousy general, had to go back to Italy and try to find land on which to settle veteran soldiers from Philippi who wanted to retire. Unfortunately, since the Triumvirs were short of money, the only way to get land was to confiscate it. The proscriptions of the previous year had brought in a lot of land, but more was needed, so various unoffending citizens were dispossessed to make way for the troops.

Naturally, such confiscations didn't make Octavian very popular in Italy. Neither did the fact that Rome's grain supply, which came mostly from overseas, was being interdicted by a fleet led by Pompey the Great's son Sextus Pompeius. Sextus' forces included ex-Pompeians, people on the proscription list, refugees from Philippi, victims of Octavian's confiscations—pretty much anyone who'd been on the losing side in any of the past ten years of conflict. Since Sextus was a good leader, he managed to put together a strong fleet and get control of several key provinces, including Sicily.

In late 41 BC, seeing that Octavian was having difficulty, Antony's wife Fulvia and his little brother Lucius Antonius, who were both hanging out in Italy, decided to collect some troops and challenge Octavian's authority. Luckily for Octavian, he had a buddy named Marcus Vipsanius Agrippa who was a much better general than him, and much better than Lucius, also, as became clear when Agrippa captured Lucius and his army early in the year 40.

Antony, meanwhile, had been settling affairs in the east, and also having an affair in the east. Since the Parthians weren't invading at the moment, he spent his time meeting with various monarchical clients and extorting money from them. One such client was Cleopatra, still queen of Egypt. She came to see Antony in Cilicia in the summer of 41. Ooh-la-la! Antony found her quite fascinating; he found her wealth and her fleet pretty fascinating too. Upon Cleopatra's invitation, he

went to visit her in late 41 and stayed all winter. He didn't get any money or ships from her, but she did end up pregnant before he left in the spring. So the winter wasn't a total loss.

The reason Antony left was that the Parthians were busily overrunning Syria. Oops! "That'll show you to spend time dallying with an ambitious temptress," said Antony's homies. But before he could deal with the Parthians, Antony heard about the troubles his relatives were causing in Italy. He hurried to Greece, where Fulvia met him and told him that he should ally with Sextus Pompeius. Antony told her to shut up and stop causing trouble, then went to Italy to make peace with Octavian so as to clear the way for a war against Parthia. While they were arranging terms, Fulvia very helpfully died, and Antony sealed his renewed friendship with Octavian by marrying the latter's sister Octavia.

Cleopatra

Now Antony was free to go fight the Parthians while Octavian tried to defeat Sextus Pompeius. As it happened, Antony, whose new wife was young and pretty, spent a few years keeping house with her and letting his subordinates drive the Parthians out of the territory they had seized. Octavian probably should have let his own subordinates handle Sextus, but Agrippa was off governing Gaul, so he tried to do it himself. In a rather comical display of military incompetence, he kept trying to sail over to Sicily, and Sextus kept sinking his ships on the way. Finally, though, Agrippa came back from Gaul and took some legions over to Sicily, where they quickly defeated Sextus' troops. Sextus himself escaped to Asia but was soon killed by one of Antony's lieutenants.

All of this took several years. Meanwhile, Antony had gotten bored with Octavia, who was mild-mannered and virtuous, and gone back to the exotic and alluring Cleopatra. In late 37 he actually married Cleopatra, which was illegal under Roman law since Cleopatra was a foreigner, plus Antony hadn't even bothered to divorce Octavia first. But bigamy was okay for Greek-speaking kings of the east, and Antony was not only personally besotted with Cleopatra, he was also excited by the idea of becoming a new King Alexander the Great, as opposed to just another Roman general.

Alexander, of course, was mostly famous for conquering the Persian Empire. The Parthians were modern-day versions of the Persians; thus, if Antony wanted to become the new Alexander, he had to finally get serious about conquering Parthia. So he saw to it that dependable client kings, like Herod the Great of Judea, were on the thrones of the various petty eastern monarchies. Then, in 36 BC, he sounded the trumpets, gathered his mighty host of eleven legions, lots of cavalry, and plenty of wagons full of food and drink, and off they all went to succeed where Crassus had failed.

Antony Heads for Parthia

Instead, they failed where Crassus had failed. The Parthians attacked the baggage train and destroyed both it and the two legions that were protecting it. Short of supplies, the Romans had to retreat. They were harassed all the way by Parthians who shot arrows at them but ran away before the Romans could get close enough to hack at them with their swords. These tactics (which the Romans thought were unsporting) had brought about Crassus' demise, but Antony was a better general than Crassus, and he had a bigger army, so he managed to get back to Syria with about two-thirds of his men still alive, if somewhat disheveled. That was enough men to keep the Parthians from counterinvading, so the war sort of fizzled out.

Sextus Pompeius dead? Parthian War over? Antony's marriage to Octavian's sister a failure? Obviously, there was nothing much to stop the two Triumvirs from fighting each other now, but first they spent a few years marshalling their forces and issuing hostile propaganda. Antony's main advantage in the eventual struggle was the wealth of the east, especially Egypt; now that she was married to him, Cleopatra was naturally willing to spend her money on his behalf. But Cleopatra also turned out to be Antony's main disadvantage, because Roman citizens didn't cotton to the idea of having a foreign queen ruling over them. So the people of Italy mostly supported Octavian. And when the two sides finally met in battle at Actium in northwest Greece in the fall of 31, large numbers of Antony's Roman troops and sailors deserted, others fought half-heartedly, and he and Cleopatra ended up fleeing to Egypt.

Foxy Cleopatra

We can't leave this section of the chapter without saying a little bit more about Cleopatra, the most famous woman of the ancient world, apart from the Virgin Mary. First off, Cleopatra wasn't Egyptian by ancestry or by culture. She was the last of a long line of Macedonian rulers of Egypt, descendants of a general of Alexander the Great. But unlike all of her predecessors, she actually took the trouble to learn to speak Egyptian, although Greek was still her mother tongue and the language used at her court.

As mentioned in the previous chapter, Cleopatra, while nice-looking enough, was not stunningly beautiful, as can be seen from the picture of her on the previous page. But she was charming enough to win over both Antony and Caesar, and to use them to help her achieve her own political ends. Whether she loved either of them is hard to say. Caesar was charming himself, and Antony was a big, strong, manly sort of guy, so maybe she fell for both of them eventually. But it was plainly their power rather than their personal qualities that attracted her to them initially.

It was rumored in ancient times that Cleopatra attempted to seduce Octavian after Antony was dead. Octavian, being a good deal less hot-blooded than Caesar or Antony, didn't go for it, so Cleopatra killed herself with the help of a venomous snake.

Octavian didn't show up in Egypt with his army until the following summer, whereat the few forces remaining to Antony and Cleopatra surrendered, and Antony and Cleopatra committed suicide. Octavian seized Cleopatra's treasure and announced that he was annexing Egypt—then paused, looked around, and said to himself, "Now what?"

Now what, indeed.

Empire!

(For optimal effect, you should pronounce the title of this section with a British accent, approximating that of *Star Trek*'s Captain Jean-Luc Picard).

Once again, Octavian had several options.

(1) Return to Italy, disband his legions, and trust the government to run things to his liking. Like Pompey had done in 62 BC. Hmm. Maybe not such a good plan.

(2) Return to Italy, use his power to reorganize the governmental system, then retire and hope that the system wouldn't fall apart. Just like Sulla. Okay, not such a great plan either.

If retirement was out of the question, then how about (3) making his autocracy official by getting himself named dictator for life, and hoping that all the senators would be happy with that plan. Same plan as Caesar had used. Also rather problematical.

The solution that Octavian came up with, after a couple of years of thinking it over, was to announce that he was laying down his powers and restoring the Republic, while simultaneously getting the Senate to name him governor of most of the frontier provinces that had legions assigned to them. Thus Octavian kept control of the military, which was the ultimate basis of his power. This "Restoration of the Republic" took place in January 27. At the same time, the Senate voted to give

Octavian a brand new name, Augustus, which means something like "the Revered." Even before he became Augustus, Octavian had taken to using the title Imperator ("Conqueror") as a name, and so did his successors. With a little warping of the Latin word imperator, we end up with the English word emperor for both Imperator Caesar Augustus and the rulers who followed him. Hence, the year 27 is now normally called not the year when the Republic was restored, but the year of the founding of the Roman Empire. (Remember to pronounce "empire" with a British accent).

Augustus pretty much ran things for the rest of his life, since regardless of his official position, all he had to do was to offer up his opinion on an issue, and the Senate, the magistrates, and the assemblies would all hasten to give that opinion the force of law. Most people were happy with the new system. Senators still got to compete for prestigious governmental positions, such as the consulship and provincial governorships. Rome's annexation of the fertile land of Egypt, along with the creation of a permanent navy for the suppression of piracy, worked to ensure that the grain supply of Rome was sufficient to keep the urban poor fed. Discharged soldiers and other land-hungry Romans were settled throughout the empire, mostly on land that Augustus bought for them from his enormous personal fortune. The equites found that peace was good for business, and that Augustus' gradual creation of a governmental bureaucracy opened up new career paths for them. Happiest of all, perhaps, were the people of the provinces, since Augustus did his best to stamp out corruption and oppression in provincial administration. And civilians everywhere were glad that the civil wars, which had been so drawn-out and bloody, were over.

Soldiers, on the other hand, might have been expected to be bored and discontented without any civil wars to fight in. Not to worry, though. One of Augustus' goals as emperor was to revive the glorious old tradition of conquering the neighbors. However, he had learned one important lesson from the past few decades: don't invade Parthia! So instead he negotiated with the Parthians, who hadn't had any more success invading Roman territory than vice versa, and got them to agree to return the legionary standards and prisoners that they'd captured over the past few decades. For many years thereafter, Rome and Parthia limited their conflicts to squabbles over whether Armenia should be a Roman client state or a Parthian one.

Closer to home, Augustus was more aggressive. To begin with, the tribes of northwestern Spain were still independent. This was embarrassing, seeing how long the Romans had been trying to conquer them, so in the mid-20's Augustus went out in person to handle the job. Apparently, he forgot that he wasn't much of a general. The fighting was arduous, and Augustus, whose health was never robust, got worn out pretty fast, so after a couple of years he declared victory and went home. Unfortunately, the Spanish didn't know that the war was over, and they kept right on fighting. Eventually, it fell to, surprise, Agrippa, to go out and finally subdue them, in 19 BC. From then on, although Augustus was still in charge of grand strategy, he left the actual fighting to his subordinates, of whom the chief, after Agrippa's death in 13 BC, were Augustus' stepsons Tiberius and Drusus.

Not just embarrassing, but actually troublesome, were the barbarian mountain people in the Alps and the Balkans, who periodically raided northern Italy, the Illyrian coast, and Macedonia. (Just like the barbarians of West Virginia who periodically raid the Washington DC area today). So they got conquered, all the way up to the Danube River. This was all so much fun that Augustus decided he should conquer the Germans in between the Rhine and Elbe Rivers as well. The Germans, however, displayed an incomprehensible lack of eagerness to enjoy the blessings of Roman rule. In 9 AD, a Germanic chieftain named Arminius ambushed and destroyed three Roman legions, and Augustus, who by now was old and tired, withdrew the rest of his forces behind the Rhine.

Despite the withdrawal, Augustus' conquests were quite impressive in the aggregate, and he had pushed the frontier so far back that Italy would be safe from foreign attackers for centuries. Plus, he had annexed Greece (to which the name "Achaea" was given), Galatia, and part of Judea, and had installed friendly client kings in places like Thrace, Mauretania, and the Bosporan kingdom north of the Black Sea. All this conquest and annexation naturally required some revamping of the provincial organization, and it took a long time to work it all out, but by 14 AD, the map looked like the one at the beginning of this chapter.

Sometime in the middle of Augustus' reign, a baby named Jesus was born in Judea, thus eventually causing the years to switch from BC to AD. Nobody in Rome paid any attention at the time.

By an amazing coincidence, 14 AD is not only the year for which that map is valid, it's also the year in which Augustus is going to die. But before he dies, we'd better mention a couple more key developments of his reign. First, the army was finally transformed into a professional organization, with soldiers who signed up for twenty-year enlistments, and who got a lump sum retirement payout in cash, rather than a grant of land. New taxes were created to pay for the new army, which was mostly distributed in the frontier provinces, except for the emperor's Praetorian Guard, which was stationed in Italy just in case anyone got any rebellious ideas. The second key development was the enhancement of Augustus' formal position in the state. Over time, he was granted the powers of a tribune for life, authority over governors of all provinces, and possibly even lifetime consular authority. In Rome, his birthday was a public holiday; in the provinces, he was worshipped as a god. In other words, it was plain by the end of Augustus' life that, his modest disclaimers notwithstanding, he was a sort of monarch.

It was further plain that he intended the monarchy to be hereditary. Having no sons of his own, he kept choosing one or another male relative as his heir. Alas, the chosen heirs kept dying. In the end, there was no good candidate left but Tiberius, son of Augustus' wife Livia by an earlier marriage. Tiberius certainly seemed like a good man for the job, based on his successful prosecution of Augustus' wars. His main defect was a marked lack of affability: apart from a few close friends, most people didn't like him very much, a feeling he fully reciprocated. Nevertheless, Augustus adopted him, and in 13 AD laws were passed giving him formal powers almost equal to those of Augustus. None too soon, since Augustus died the next year at the age of seventy-seven. Not bad for a man who was sickly for his whole life.

Augustus the Great?

As I may have mentioned already (yeah, only about a dozen times), Augustus was not much of a soldier. Nor does he seem to have been a brilliant orator, a great writer, or even a very good dancer. Although I'm not sure about that last one—maybe he was a regular Fred Astaire, but he just chose not to dance in public. Anyway, the point is, he didn't have all the talents of his adoptive father Gaius Julius, yet he succeeded in establishing a popular and successful form of government that endured long after his death.

How did he do it? Well, among other things, he came to power early and lived a long time. Note to all you would-be emperors out there: you're more likely to make a lasting impact if you don't get yourself assassinated within a year of becoming dictator for life. Not that longevity in and of itself guarantees success. Kim Il-Sung ruled North Korea for about half a century and succeeded in running it almost completely into the ground.

Unlike Kim, luckily, Augustus was neither megalomaniacal nor devoted to an idiotic economic theory. He could be ruthless when it served his purpose, especially in his youth, as when he joined with Antony and Lepidus in the proscriptions of 42 BC. But once he became emperor, he preferred to win over potential opponents in the upper classes by making them partners in his rule. Rome's expanded empire needed a lot of governing, after all, and Augustus couldn't attend to everything personally. So senators could aspire to magistracies which retained some of their old functions and almost all of their old prestige. Additionally, ex-magistrates could still serve as governors of provinces, either as Augustus' lieutenants or under their own flag. And since Augustus had arranged for governors to draw a regular salary, they were now less likely to plunder the people whom they were supposed to be administering. Lastly, Augustus established a variety of governmental agencies, including a police force, a fire brigade, and a grain commission for the city of Rome. These agencies were always headed by senators or equestrians nominated by the emperor.

All these measures show not only that Augustus wanted the support of the upper classes, but also that he was interested in the welfare of the common man. Also the common woman, presumably, although like most Romans of his day, he probably thought of the common woman principally as an adjunct of the common man. Likewise, the common child. Anyway, the common man recognized that Augustus had done a lot more for him than the Senate was likely to, so he was more than willing to see republican pseudo-democracy give way to imperial quasi-monarchy. The soldiers, too, were solidly behind the imperial system that had brought them clear terms of service and a guaranteed retirement payout.

Young Octavian, Trying
Hard to Look Like a Soldier

What sort of man was Augustus? It's hard to say, because his iconic status, both at the time and later on, worked to conceal his private nature. His public life showed that he was shrewd, cautious, calculating, unostentatious, hard-working, fair-minded, practical, and dedicated to the welfare of his country and its people. A lover of tradition, he disapproved of the libertinism of the Roman upper classes and was a devoted husband to Livia. On the other hand, he wasn't such a successful father: his only child, a daughter named Julia, rebelled against his old-fashioned morality and became notorious for her extramarital affairs.

So family life wasn't a bundle of joy for the emperor, given his daughter's behavior and the way his designated heirs kept dying off. But whatever his private sorrows, he had all of the following accomplishments to his credit: he formed a more perfect union, established justice, ensured domestic tranquillity, provided for the common defense, and, not least, promoted the general welfare. True, he didn't secure the blessings of liberty to the Romans and their posterity, but five out of six ain't bad.

Culture, Anyone?

Whoo-ee, doggies! Them Romans sho did get theyselves a whole heap o' culture when big ole Gus was emperor. Uh-huh.

Sorry. I lapsed into my native, relatively uncultured dialect for a minute there. I do that sometimes when I'm contemplating a culture higher than my own. (My own cultural activities are mostly limited to watching football and reading the Sunday comics). But the fact remains that Roman fine arts and literature flourished in the first century BC, especially once Augustus brought internal peace to the Mediterranean world.

Augustus himself was particularly proud of all the temples and other public buildings that he constructed in Rome, or repaired, in the case of tumble-down older structures. He once said, "I found Rome brick and left it marble," which could have been a metaphorical comment about the state of the commonwealth, but was also literally true in that he plunked down marble buildings all over the place. His close collaborators did likewise. Especially Agrippa. The best preserved of all of these buildings is the Pantheon, a former temple that you can still visit in Rome today. There's a big inscription on the front that says, "Built by Marcus Agrippa, son of Lucius, in his third consulship." Actually, Agrippa's structure was almost completely rebuilt by a later emperor in the year 120 AD, so only the front porch is Agrippa's work, but it's still got his name on it. The Pantheon is in excellent shape today because it was well built in the first place and has been in continuous use ever since 120, meaning that people have made repairs to it as necessary over the years.

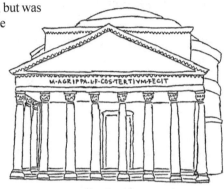

The Pantheon

All this construction, which Augustus and friends funded out of their own pockets (full of loot from Egypt and elsewhere), naturally provided lots of jobs for laborers, building contractors, engineers, architects, interior decorators, and so on. So did the building of new roads and other public works projects. Thus, the architectural beautification of Rome not only made everyone feel proud of the city, it also helped contribute to economic prosperity.

Smaller scale art also did well in the late Republic and early empire. Portrait sculpture came into its own, as mentioned last chapter. Wealthy Romans eagerly paid top dollar not just for portrait busts, but for sculptures and paintings of all kinds. Fancy table settings, elaborate clothing, and exquisite jewelry also were popular, to the annoyance of Augustus, who, like Cato, regarded such things as frivolous.

From the modern American point of view, a lot of this art and architecture is inaccessible, since much of it has faded or fallen apart, and what's left is mostly in Europe, which is hard to get to by car. On the other hand, Roman literature also flourished in the first century BC, and such literature as has not been lost is perfectly accessible as long as you can read Latin. What? You can't read Latin? Well, luckily, it's almost all available in English translation, although a lot of the texts make for better reading in the original.

Here's a brief rundown of the top writers of the late Republic and early empire:

Cicero: We've met him already. Wrote speeches, philosophy, essays, and letters. A brilliant stylist, often regarded as the model for refined Latin prose.

Caesar: Wrote histories of his own wars as propaganda exercises. Clear, effective prose writer.

Catullus: Younger contemporary of Cicero and Caesar, most famous for lyric poems about love and despair, which went together then just like they do now. Died young. How tragic.

Sallust: Grouchy ex-Caesarian, forced into retirement for corruption, wrote monographs about Jugurtha and Catiline. Purposefully old-fashioned style makes for difficult but rewarding reading.

Vergil: Author of the *Aeneid*, an epic about a mythological ancestor of Augustus. The *Aeneid* is one of the greatest pieces of literature ever written, and if you haven't read it yet, do so. As soon as you're done with this book, that is.

Horace: Like Vergil, wrote during Augustus' reign. Outstanding lyric poet, genial, often humorous, sometimes serious, always enjoyable.

Livy: We've met him already, too. On good terms personally with Augustus, but nostalgic for the old Republic. Good storyteller, competent if unexciting stylist.

Ovid: Wrote poems on mythological topics. Also wrote a how-to pamphlet on adultery. Augustus was not amused.

By the way, that's not really my native dialect at the top of this page. I was born in Minnesota. Minnesotans don't say "Whoo-ee!"

Review Questions for Chapter Five

1. Have you noticed that I think pretty highly of Augustus? No? Well, try to pay more attention in the future.

2. Can you guess which month of our modern calendar was named in honor of Augustus? *Hint: it comes right after July and shortly before September.*

3. Can you guess why Augustus chose to have the month previously called Sextilis named after him?
    (a) It was the month of his birth.
    (b) It was the month when he first assumed the consulship.
    (c) It was the month when he annexed Egypt.
    (d) All of the above.
    (e) All of the above except (a). Not counting (d) as one of the above, though.
    Hint: Augustus was born in September. And (e) is a better answer than (b) or (c).

4. Do you think Cleopatra was a good queen?
    (a) Yes.
    (b) No.
    (c) How should I know? This book hasn't told me anything about her rule in Egypt.
    (d) Yes, up until the time when she got her country conquered by Octavian. Oops.

5. Did you notice, on the map at the beginning of the chapter, that Cisalpine Gaul is no longer a province, but has been incorporated into Italy, with full citizenship rights and everything? You did notice? Well done! Here, have a cookie.

Strange Interlude

Act One (numerological):

Number 1—The larch. The larch.
Number 9...Number 9...Number 9...
Who are you?
The new Number 2.
Who is Number 1?
You are Number 6.
I am not a number. I am a free man.
Yeah, right.

Part Two (categorical):

Are too!
Am not!
Are too!
Am not!
Are too!
Am not!
Are too!

Section Three (controversial):

To advance such a viewpoint, of course, is to invite scorn and ridicule, if not worse, from one's fellow scientists, all of them adhering to an orthodoxy which cannot easily be challenged, insofar as it is upon that very orthodoxy that their own position of established authority depends. Nevertheless, such claims will not be so automatically dismissed by those scholars, who, abandoning the hypothesis-laden atmosphere of the workshop, venture to test their ideas by exposing them to the raw data derived from new and innovative and groundbreaking and pretty darned exciting research.

Chapter Four (immaterial):

PIE *$\hat{g}enh_2us$ 'jaw, cheek, chin'
    a. Skt. *hánu-* 'jaw'
    b. Gk. *génus* 'jaw, cheek', *gnáthos/gnathmós* 'jaw, cheek', *géneion* 'chin', Lat. *genuīnus* 'molar', *gena* 'cheek', Goth. *kinnus* 'cheek', OE *cinn* 'chin', Arm. *cnawt* 'cheek, jaw'
    c. Av. *zanu-* 'jaw', Lith. *žándas* 'jaw', OIr *giun* 'mouth', Toch. A *śanwem* 'jaws (dual)'

THE HISTORY OF ROME

Chapter Six

*in which there are several tyrannical emperors, three yellowish emperors,
and one year with four different emperors*

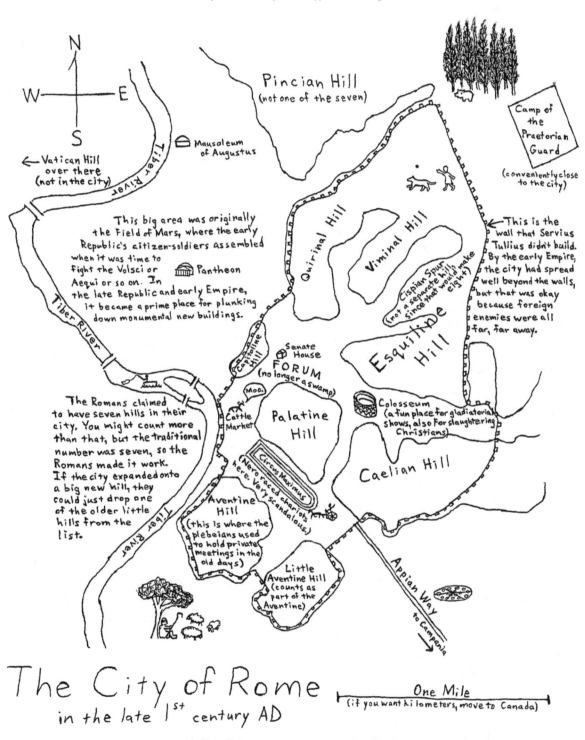

N
W — E
S

Pincian Hill
(not one of the seven)

Tiber River

Mausoleum of Augustus

← Vatican Hill over there (not in the city)

Camp of the Praetorian Guard

(conveniently close to the city)

This big area was originally the Field of Mars, where the early Republic's citizen-soldiers assembled when it was time to fight the Volsci or Aequi or so on. In the late Republic and early Empire, it became a prime place for plunking down monumental new buildings.

Pantheon

Quirinal Hill

Viminal Hill

Cispian Spur (not a separate hill, since that would make eight)

Esquiline Hill

← This is the wall that Servius Tullius didn't build. By the early Empire, the city had spread well beyond the walls, but that was okay because foreign enemies were all far, far away.

Tiber River

Capitoline Hill

Senate House

FORUM (no longer a swamp)

Moo.

Cattle Market

Palatine Hill

Colosseum (a fun place for gladiatorial shows, also for slaughtering Christians)

The Romans claimed to have seven hills in their city. You might count more than that, but the traditional number was seven, so the Romans made it work. If the city expanded onto a big new hill, they could just drop one of the older little hills from the list.

Caelian Hill

Circus Maximus (Nero raced chariots here. Very scandalous.)

Tiber River

Aventine Hill (this is where the plebeians used to hold private meetings in the old days)

Little Aventine Hill (counts as part of the Aventine)

Appian Way

to Campania

The City of Rome
in the late 1st century AD

One Mile
(if you want kilometers, move to Canada)

A group of academic historians made an unannounced visit to my house late last night. They said that they had spent decades trying to get history accepted as a science, and that it would be a good idea if I cut back on the detailed information about famous individuals, and threw in some dry analysis of sociohistorical trends. If I failed to concur, they said, bad things might happen. "What sort of things?" I asked. "Bad things," said one of them, knocking over and stomping on my beloved Hummel figurine of a gnome eating a squirrel. "Hey, my Aunt Stella gave me that," I cried out. "Ain't that sweet," he replied. "Everyone should have an Aunt Stella. Be a shame if anything was to happen to yours."

Before they left, I promised to include at least a little bit of impersonal history in this chapter. But don't worry, there'll still be a good bit of stuff about famous individuals. After all, what would an empire be without emperors?

Also expect charts and graphs. They said I needed fewer pictures of famous people, and more charts and graphs.

The Julio-Claudian Emperors

Tiberius came to the throne as a gloomy-minded middle-aged man, and his life as emperor just made him gloomier. Throughout his reign, he worked conscientiously to keep the empire secure and prosperous, but still the Senate and the urban populace didn't love him. Eventually, he got sick of Rome and moved to the resort island of Capri, where, according to hostile later legend, he whiled away his time taking private baths with small boys. Meanwhile, he had left the prefect of the Praetorian Guard, Lucius Aelius Sejanus, in charge in the capital. Sejanus, who liked being in charge, started getting rid of Tiberius' meddlesome family members by persuading the suspicious old man that they were plotting against him. After several years, though, the suspicious old man turned his suspicions on Sejanus and had him executed. It was unfortunate for everyone, though no one realized it at the time, that Sejanus had not yet had time to get rid of Tiberius' grandnephew Gaius, nicknamed Caligula, who became the heir apparent.

> Sometime toward the end of Tiberius' reign, Jesus was executed in Judea on suspicion of being a troublemaker. No one in Rome paid any attention at the time.

In the provinces, Tiberius installed competent governors and let them deal with the few local rebellions that cropped up. His inherent pessimism convinced him that Germany wasn't worth the lives, expense, and considerable risk that would be involved in conquering it, so he left the frontier at the Rhine. In the east, though, he annexed Cappadocia and a couple of smaller client states when their respective kings died. The annexations involved little cost or effort but promised to increase imperial revenues. Tiberius was fond of revenue.

Tiberius died in 37 AD. In Rome, Senate and people alike rejoiced at the departure of the dour old miser and looked forward to the reign of the youthful Caligula. Too bad Caligula turned out to be tyrannical and incompetent, not to mention depraved and megalomaniacal. Eager for glory, he made grandiose plans to conquer Germany and Britain but chickened out at the last minute. Closer to home, his spendthrift ways led him to impose new taxes and to confiscate the estates of wealthy senators. Soon there were plots against him, which led him to start executing suspected plotters left and right, which only caused more people to start plotting. In 41 AD, one of the plots succeeded, and Caligula was assassinated at the age of 29.

Understandably after such a reign, the Senate now considered abolishing the empire altogether and restoring rule by the consuls. However, the Praetorian Guard, whose job was to protect the emperor, naturally preferred finding another Caesar to being unemployed. The only adult male member of the imperial family who was still around after all the executions was Caligula's uncle Claudius, a 50-year-old pedant whom everyone from Augustus onward had regarded as seriously lacking in good sense. Still, beggars can't be choosers, so the praetorians hailed Claudius as emperor and urged the Senate to do likewise. Noting that the praetorians were heavily armed, the Senate quickly complied.

Claudius tried hard to be a good emperor by getting personally involved in the details of administration. However, the Senate never liked him. Most senators found his personal eccentricities distasteful and resented the fact that he had been forced on them by the army. In turn, Claudius suspected many senators of disloyalty and occasionally had the suspects executed.

Thus, Claudius was more openly dependent on the army's good will than Augustus and Tiberius had been. He prudently gave a large cash gift to the praetorians upon his accession, unfortunately causing them to expect similar gifts from every future new emperor. To win the respect of the army as a whole, he decided to conquer Britain. The Britons weren't threatening to invade or anything, but Claudius wanted to conquer somebody, and the Britons seemed like easier pickings than the redoubtable Germans. An army of four legions dutifully attacked the main kingdom in southeastern Britain; then, when most of the fighting was done, Claudius himself hastened up from Rome to "take command" of the army as it captured the enemy capital.

Elsewhere, Claudius annexed Lycia because it seemed silly for it to still be independent. He also annexed Mauretania, whose king had been murdered by Caligula for some bizarre reason. Finally, he annexed Thrace and the non-Roman parts of Judea when their kings died. Apparently, he liked annexing people.

Claudius married four times in his life. His last wife, Agrippina, was also his niece, making the marriage incestuous and illegal under Roman law, but Claudius was emperor, so he wasn't arrested. Marrying Agrippina was a bad idea, though. She had a son by a previous marriage, and, once she got Claudius to adopt him, she poisoned her husband, in the year 54, so as to bring her son to the throne.

The son, whose name after adoption was Nero, was a spoiled 16-year-old who liked music, art, theater, Greek culture, and late-night carousing with dissolute young noblemen. Early on, he devoted himself to his amusements and let his advisers, including the philosopher and playwright Lucius Annaeus Seneca, run the government. Seneca and friends treated the Senate respectfully and stopped executing people so often. During this period, the conquest of Britain ground forward

A Mauretanian Reacts to the News that He's Been Annexed

65

slowly, Rome and Parthia got into a war over Armenia, and the empire was administered competently.

As Nero got older, though, he became interested in running things himself. He also got annoyed with his attractive and domineering mother, who disapproved of his having girlfriends (Dr. Freud, we have a patient for you). Eventually, he had his mother killed (Dr. Freud, where are you?) and told Seneca that it was time to retire. He also began giving concerts and acting on the public stage, and taking part in chariot races. To Romans with traditional values, being an entertainer/athlete was almost as scandalous as matricide, and opposition to the emperor mounted. Aware of the opposition, Nero spent the rest of his reign executing evergrowing numbers of suspected plotters, including his onetime father figure Seneca (just forget about it, Dr. Freud, you should have come the first time we called).

In 64, there was a disastrous fire at Rome. Nero's reputation had sunk so low that he was widely believed to have started it deliberately so that he could begin an urban renewal program. Desperate to deflect popular anger, the emperor decided to blame the fire on the Christians, a strange new religious sect with a bad reputation. As a side benefit, Nero got to amuse himself by dreaming up gruesome new ways of executing Christians in the arena. In the long run, though, the fortitude with which Christians faced torture and death won them quite a few admirers among the general public.

But back to Nero. He annexed the Roman client state in the Alps, tried but failed to annex Armenia, and in general oppressed the provinces, thus provoking a major revolt in Judea in 66. He also spent so much on things like building himself a palace that he didn't have enough money to pay the legions regularly (this last lapse showing that in the final analysis, he just wasn't all that bright). In 68, provincial governors in Gaul and Spain rebelled, and Nero realized that his only significant supporters were the Praetorian Guard and the urban poor, who had benefited from his extravagant spending. But then, seeing which way the wind was blowing, the praetorians deserted Nero in hopes of getting a substantial cash gift from the rebellious Spanish governor, who was now proclaimed emperor. Nero, in despair, committed suicide, one of the few worthwhile things he'd ever done.

> ### Jews and Christians
>
> Romans didn't like Jews much, because Jews, unlike people from other provinces, refused to worship the emperors as gods, and indeed denied that any of the Roman gods were real. This attitude hurt the Romans' feelings. More importantly, a refusal by provincials to worship the emperor seemed like evidence of rebellious tendencies.
>
> Christians, whose numbers increased fairly rapidly after the death of Jesus, were initially regarded as somewhat deviant Jews who hated the secular world and held bizarre secret meetings involving ritual cannibalism. But the Christians were active proselytizers, so that over time, more and more non-Jews became Christians. Eventually, Christianity came to be seen as an independent religion, though still deviant and probably seditious.

Thus ended the Julio-Claudian dynasty, so called (in case you were wondering) because it claimed descent from Julius Caesar and from Tiberius' father, who was one of the many Claudii of Roman history. It ended because Nero, a decadent Greek-loving singer and actor who never bothered to take part in military campaigns himself, lost the support of both the troops and their generals. When it came time to overthrow him, it turned out that successive emperors had killed off so many of their own relatives that there weren't any Julio-Claudians left to take the throne. That didn't mean there would be an end to the empire, though. The troops knew that emperors, being dependent on military support, would treat them much better than a republic would. If a Julio-Claudian wasn't available, they'd just have to choose someone else.

Citizens, Soldiers, Senators, Caesars

All right, all right, I'll say something about broad sociohistorical developments now. First off, citizens. From the end of the Republic onward, the people of Italy, including what used to be Cisalpine Gaul, were all citizens. Except slaves and foreign immigrants, of course; the Romans didn't regard *those* sorts of people as worthy of citizenship. Moreover, not only did growing numbers of Roman citizens settle in the provinces, where they could get cheap land, but the emperors also passed out citizenship pretty freely to non-Italians. Citizenship no longer meant that you got to help choose consuls and other magistrates, since the emperors eventually took to just appointing people for those jobs. But it did give you prestige, and also certain special rights in areas such as court proceedings and taxation.

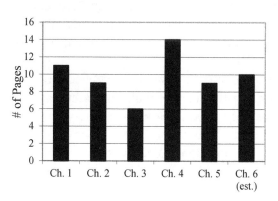

Graph Indicating the Number of Pages per Chapter in this Book So Far

Citizens also had the exclusive privilege of serving in the legions. It was just as well, then, that there were lots of citizens in places like northern Italy and Gaul, because the people of central and southern Italy, economically well-off and no longer in danger from foreign invasion, weren't enthusiastic about signing up for a twenty-year hitch on the Rhine or Danube. (The Praetorian Guard, which got higher pay and was stationed just outside Rome, was a different matter: most praetorians were from central Italy). Even citizens from Gaul didn't want to serve way out east, though, plus there were fewer citizens in general in the eastern provinces. Thus, to ensure sufficient legionary manpower on the Parthian border, Galatians, Syrians, and so on were often given immediate citizenship in return for enlistment.

Most non-citizens couldn't sneak into the legions through that loophole. However, they could still become auxiliaries, that is, non-citizen soldiers with Roman officers. Auxiliaries got paid less than legionaries, and they had to serve for twenty-five years instead of just twenty, but upon retirement, they got both citizenship and a cash bonus. The auxiliaries were an important part of the army; in particular, they provided light infantry and cavalry to complement the legionary heavy infantry.

Being a soldier, although it was often toilsome and sometimes hazardous, gave you a sort of privileged position as long as there was an emperor around. The ultimate basis of imperial authority was the military. Naturally, then, emperors tried to win the favor of the soldiers, often by handing out substantial cash gifts to the rank and file.

Emperors also kept a watchful eye on high-ranking military officers, especially legionary commanders and provincial governors, who were usually senators. The Senate might not be in charge of the state anymore, but individual senators were still wealthy and influential. Indeed, the emperors helped to keep the Senate prestigious by incorporating leading men from the Italian towns, and later from the provinces, into its ranks. Since senators still filled lots of important administrative positions, it made sense to admit qualified men of non-Roman ancestry. The downside, of course, was that capable, wealthy, influential senators in key administrative or military positions were always a potential threat to the emperor. Thus, the Caesars gradually took to bypassing the official magistrates and relying more and more on their own privately appointed servants as administrators.

Likewise, the Senate as a body quickly lost its legislative authority and became just a rubber stamp for imperial edicts.

Foolish emperors, noting the weakness of the Senate as an institution and the servility of most of its members, often treated it contemptuously. Big mistake. The Senate generally had to approve of whomever the troops favored as new emperor, but senators could and did plot against emperors who offended them. Even when plots failed, the inevitable retribution just fostered increased discontent and further plotting, as we've already seen in the Julio-Claudian period.

So, a wise Caesar flattered the Senate by giving jobs to its more illustrious members and politely asking for advice from the body as a whole. Nevertheless, as time went on, the emperors became more and more openly monarchical, with palaces, court intrigues, and all the other stuff that makes monarchies so much fun to read about in the tabloids. By the time Nero committed suicide, everyone was so used to having an emperor that there was no question of restoring the old republican constitution. The only issue was who would succeed Nero now that the Julio-Claudian line was tapped out.

Before we find that out, though, I suppose I should mention something else about the emperors. I called them Caesars in the title of this section mostly because it alliterated nicely with the other words in the title. But now it would behoove me to explain that Caesar, which was originally just a family name, developed under the early empire into a sort of title for any emperor, regardless of his ancestry. That's why the Russians and Germans later called their emperors Czars and Kaisers, respectively. Apparently, Russians and Germans don't know how to spell very well.

The Year of Four Emperors

And now, back to our story. In 68 AD, the Senate confirmed the accession to the throne of the rebel Spanish governor, Servius Sulpicius Galba. Galba was a childless 73-year-old senator whose main concern, once he reached Rome, was to put a stop to the profligate governmental expenditure of Nero's last years. Unfortunately, his refusal to pay the expected monetary bonus to the praetorians made them susceptible to the blandishments of his disaffected lieutenant, Marcus Salvius Otho. Otho, as governor of Lusitania, had supported Galba's rebellion, and he was upset when Galba refused to name him heir apparent. So in January 69, Otho bribed the praetorians, had Galba killed, and got the Senate to announce that he was the new emperor.

If Otho had known that the year 69 was going to be called The Year of Four Emperors, maybe he wouldn't have volunteered to be the second of them. Nor would a fat, lazy general on the Rhine have decided to become the third. The general in question, Aulus Vitellius, a senator of distinguished parentage, was popular with his troops because he was good-natured and a lax disciplinarian. He himself was more interested in eating and drinking than in starting a rebellion, but two of his subordinates were more ambitious. Most importantly, the legionaries saw no reason why they shouldn't get their own candidate on the throne, in place of Galba, Spain's favorite son. Vitellius was willing enough to gratify them, provided his subordinates did most of the work.

Thus, Otho soon heard that, shortly before Galba's death, the Rhine army had declared Vitellius emperor and started marching south. Poor Otho, surprised to find anyone rebelling against him before he had even begun to reign, nevertheless collected what troops he could in Italy and marched north to the Po Valley. The Danube legions, loyal to Otho, started marching to join him, but the Vitellians beat them to northern Italy and defeated Otho's outnumbered troops. Otho, who had never expected to get into a civil war, decided to prevent further bloodshed by conceding defeat and committing suicide. A noble thing to do, though in fact he didn't prevent further bloodshed, since there was still one more emperor to come.

Vitellius himself had not even reached northern Italy when the battle was fought and won by his two energetic lieutenants. When he finally got to Rome, where of course the Senate had ratified his emperorship, he spent a lot of time feasting while his undisciplined troops complained about the heat. Soon, the troops and generals in the east decided that they could come up with a better emperor than Vitellius. The man they settled on was Titus Flavius Vespasianus, an ex-consul with a solid military record who was busy trying to repress the Jewish revolt that had begun under Nero. The Danube legions, unhappy that Vitellius had beaten Otho before they had even gotten into the game, decided to support Vespasian. In fact, without even waiting for Vespasian to leave the east, the Danube legions charged into northern Italy, where they met and defeated

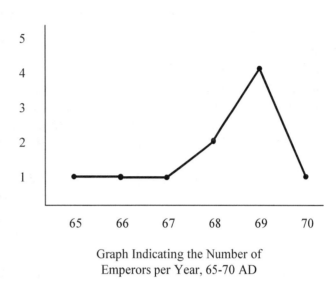

Graph Indicating the Number of Emperors per Year, 65-70 AD

Vitellius' army in late October. Vitellius, who characteristically had stayed in Rome while his men were dying up north, tried to abdicate when the Danube legions approached the city in late December. But his own remaining troops wouldn't let him quit, so the Danubians stormed the city, and Vitellius was captured and killed. Thus Vespasian became the fourth and last emperor of the year 69.

The Yellowish Emperors

Vespasian's dynasty is called Flavian, from the family name Flavius, meaning yellowish. (China's legendary founder also happens to be called the called the Yellow Emperor. Not that that's relevant to anything.) Vespasian is one of my favorite emperors, and not just because he looks a little like my paternal grandfather. So, at the risk of having my tires slashed by an irate academic historian, I'm going to include a portrait of him along with my description of his reign. See, there it is, just to the left of this sentence.

As you might guess from his picture, Vespasian was an unostentatious, practical sort of man with a wry sense of humor. He was one of those small-town Italians whom previous emperors had promoted into the Senate because they looked like they'd make good government officials. Good officials like Vespasian had kept the government running tolerably well even when emperors were acting goofy. Now that he was in charge himself, Vespasian's first priority was stabilizing a military situation

Vespasian

that had been shaken by the civil war. An uprising by auxiliaries on the Rhine was suppressed, and Vespasian's son Titus, who'd been left in command in Judea when Dad sailed off to become emperor, captured Jerusalem, thus effectively ending the Jewish revolt. Next it was

69

time to press northward in Britain, and to annex a few of the minor client states in Asia Minor that hadn't been annexed so far. Also, Vespasian must have had a map similar to the one at the beginning of Chapter Five, because he noticed that the frontier in central Europe would be shorter if he seized the triangle of land between the upper reaches of the Rhine and the Danube. So he, or rather, his generals and soldiers, seized it.

At home, the imperial finances were in dire straits. So Vespasian increased tax rates and created new taxes as well, such as one on public toilets. Said tax led to one of the witty remarks for which Vespasian was well known: on being asked if he wasn't embarrassed to be taxing toilets, he held up a coin and said, "The money doesn't smell." All this taxation annoyed people, of course; what else is new? But Vespasian spent the money wisely, on military pay and public works like building the Colosseum (though it wasn't finished till a couple of years after his death), as well as on helping out senators and equites who got into financial difficulties. Capable government, combined with Vespasian's cheerful, down-to-earth personality, made him a popular emperor and ensured a smooth succession for Titus when his father died in 79 AD.

Titus was handsome, friendly, generous, a successful general, and an experienced vice-emperor. He ended up being one of the most popular emperors of Roman history, but maybe that's just because he died before the honeymoon was over. After all, Caligula and Nero were popular at first also. The gods didn't

Famous Last Words

The Senate had a habit of voting posthumous divine honors to emperors whom it liked, in imitation of the divinity voted to Caesar after his death. Vespasian, knowing that Titus would make sure of his deification, made a famous quip when death was drawing near him: "Alas, I think I'm becoming a god." Later, feeling himself slipping away, he asked his attendants to help him out of bed, saying, "An emperor should die standing." He didn't die standing, though; the struggle to rise was too much for him, and he expired in his attendants' arms. The Senate voted to make him a god anyway.

seem too fond of Titus: during his two-year reign, Mt. Vesuvius erupted, burying tens of thousands of people in Pompeii and nearby towns, while Rome was ravaged by both an epidemic and another big fire. Luckily, a great many Romans no longer believed in the traditional gods, and Titus in fact

Pompeii

When Mt. Vesuvius erupted in 79 AD, it completely buried the small city of Pompeii. Archeologists started digging it up again a few hundred years ago, and now you can go visit it if you want to see what everyday life was like in a Roman municipality. Too bad so many people had to die, but what the heck, none of them were personal friends of ours.

became all the more popular by spending a lot of money to help out the victims of these disasters.

Then he died in the year 81, and since he had no children, his little brother Domitian took the throne. Domitian, the neglected younger son, may have had an inferiority complex; at any rate, he liked to order people around and to be addressed as "Lord and God." Early in his reign, he just ignored the Senate. But after an abortive rebellion by a general along the Rhine in 89 AD, Domitian realized that his despotic tendencies had led to disloyalty, so he figured he'd better start executing disaffected senators and army officers. By the year 93, he was executing people at an alarmingly high rate. High enough, anyway, to alarm the commanders of the Praetorian Guard, as well as Domitian's own wife, who suspected that they might be next on the list. (His wife had not always been faithful to her marriage vows, and she knew that he knew it). So in 96, they assassinated him, and since Domitian had no children, the Flavian dynasty came to an end. And not a moment too soon, seeing as we've reached the bottom of this page.

Pick a God, any God

As mentioned earlier in this chapter, Romans of the early empire tended to fall away from their old-time religion, which seemed impersonal and lacking in spiritual uplift. Luckily, contact with the cultures of the eastern Mediterranean gave them access to lots of more personally involving faiths. Here are some of the major deities that they could choose from.

Cybele, a.k.a. The Great Mother. Originally an earth goddess from Asia Minor, Cybele liked banging on a kettle drum and riding around on a cart drawn by lions. She also liked her male devotees to castrate themselves; not surprisingly, more women than men chose to become her followers. Her major ritual involved slaughtering a bull and drenching people with its blood. Yuck.

> *Pros:* Exciting ceremonies that induced religious ecstasy
> *Cons:* Castration and general yuckiness

Isis. An ancient Egyptian goddess (but she changed her hair and dress style when she moved to Rome), Isis promised healing to the sick and life after death to the devout. She preferred hand-held noisemakers to drums and didn't favor castration. Her worship involved secret initiation rites in which the initiate was supposed to experience transcendental union with the divine powers.

> *Pros:* Life after death, allure of ancient Egyptian wisdom
> *Cons:* Conservative Romans frowned upon powerful Egyptian women
> (cf. Cleopatra)

Mithras. A god of Persian origin, Mithras was a good-guy warrior in the battle between light and darkness. He was famous for killing a bull, a long long time ago. Mithraism reminds me of the modern-day Shriners: the god wore a funny hat and short cape, while his worshippers were all men and advanced through several degrees of Mithraism. Mithras was popular with soldiers and businessmen.

> *Pros (for men):* No women allowed
> *Cons (for women):* No women allowed

YHWH the Lord. The god of Israel. A stern fellow who demanded ethical behavior from his people and made long lists of rules to help them know what ethical behavior was. His worshippers said that he was the only true god, and that he didn't like it when people worshipped other, non-existent gods. In the late Republic and early empire, Jews moved from Judea all over the Roman world, taking their religion with them, and winning many converts among Romans and non-Romans alike.

NO PICTURES ALLOWED

> *Pros:* Detailed code of ethics attracted people who wanted to live upright lives but
> weren't always sure how
> *Cons:* Lots of rules to remember, circumcision required of male converts, denial of
> other gods annoyed non-Jews

Jesus Christ. Said by his followers to be the divine son of YHWH, risen from the dead after crucifixion. Like YHWH, denied the existence of foreign gods; said he alone was the path to salvation. Demanded upright behavior but stressed the spirit rather than the letter of the law, hence didn't require circumcision. Promised eternal bliss to the faithful after his return at some unspecified future date.

> *Pros:* High ethical standards, promise of eternal bliss, no circumcision
> *Cons:* Christianity was illegal: adherents were subject to arrest and possible
> execution

Review Questions for Chapter Six

1. Why do you suppose I never told you a two or three word name for emperors like Claudius and Domitian, after I made a big deal in an earlier chapter about Roman nomenclature?

   (a) I'm lazy.

   (b) That's what everyone else does.

   (c) Emperors who inherited their position in the 1st century normally had lots of extra names, just like English royalty does today, and no one bothers to remember all of Claudius' names any more than anyone bothers to remember that Prince Charles is officially named Charles Philip Arthur George Windsor.

   (d) All of the above.

2. On p. 70, when I mentioned finances and dire straits in the same sentence, did you think of the song "Money for Nothing"?

3. Consider the chart below, which shows important information about the ten emperors in this chapter, then answer the questions below.

Name	Years of Reign	Died of Natural Causes?	Posthumously Deified?
Tiberius	14-37	probably[1]	no
Caligula	37-41	no[2]	no[3]
Claudius	41-54	no[4]	yes
Nero	54-68	no[5]	no[6]
Galba	68-69	no[2]	no
Otho	69	no[5]	no
Vitellius	69	no[2]	no
Vespasian	69-79	yes	yes
Titus	79-81	probably[1]	yes
Domitian	81-96	no[2]	no

Notes:
[1] Rumored to have been poisoned by successor; rumors probably not true.
[2] Killed by multiple hack and/or stab wounds.
[3] Yeah, right, as if.
[4] Poisoned by his wife.
[5] Committed suicide by stabbing self with a dagger.
[6] If it had been up to the Greeks, they would have deified him.

   a) Would you have wanted to be emperor, given the high risk of violent death and the odds against deification?

   b) Do you think that there've been enough charts and graphs in this chapter that I won't have to include them in the next chapter unless I want to?

Answers: 1. (d)

2. Well, I did even if you didn't.

3.a) Yes, you would have, because you're incurably ambitious.

 b) Well, I think so, and that's what matters.

Poetic Interlude

Beginning in the late Republic, Roman citizens began to settle more and frequently in the provinces. At first, their colonies were islands of Romanness (Romanship? Romanhood?) in seas of foreignosity. But over the generations, the colonists' descendants grew up among and intermarried with the locals, while citizenship, Roman culture, and the Latin language became widespread throughout the population, at least in the western half of the empire. Anyway, the poem below is expressive of the changing sensibilities of the settlers' descendants.

The land was ours before we were the land's.

She was our land more than a hundred years

Before we were her people. She was ours

In Gaul and Spain, in Africa as well,

But we were Italy's, still colonials,

Possessing what we still were unpossessed by,

Possessed by what we now no more possessed.

Something we were withholding from the land

Until we found out that it was our culture

We were withholding from our land of ruling,

And so we sought to transform all the locals.

Such as they were, we changed to be like us

(We'd earned that right through many deeds of war).

Thus is the land vaguely Romanizing westward,

But still half-foreign, halfway unenhanced,

Such is she now, but Roman she'll become.

(with apologies to Robert Frost)

THE HISTORY OF ROME

Chapter Seven

in which there are five good emperors, plus one not-so-good co-emperor who, luckily, doesn't really count

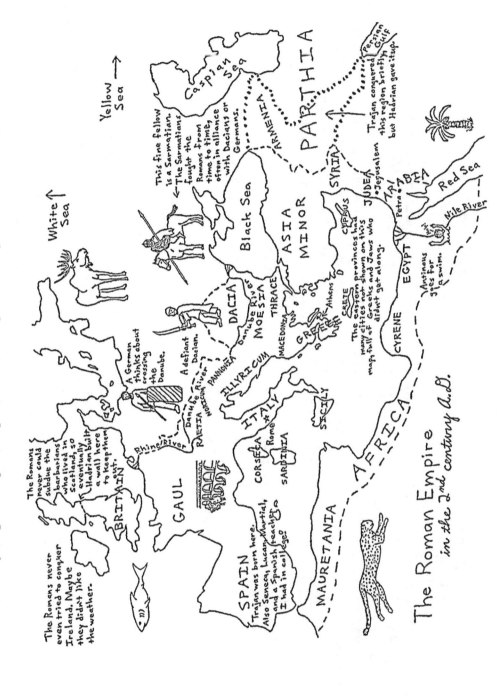

The Roman Empire
in the 2nd century A.D.

Five Good Emperors in a Row
(what are the odds?)

I can't prove that the leaders of the Senate had advance knowledge of the plot to kill Domitian, but it sure didn't take them long to nominate a successor once they heard of Domitian's death. Like about five seconds. The man they chose was Marcus Cocceius Nerva, an elderly, childless senator, well-liked by his fellow nobles, but not so popular with the army, given his lack of military experience. The Senate named Nerva emperor, but by 97 AD there was muttering in the ranks. Nerva, not wanting to be hacked to death by his own troops, decided to adopt an heir. His choice was Marcus Trajan in English, a Spanish-born general and ex-consul currently commanding an army along the Rhine. And an excellent choice he turned out to be.

Nerva died in early 98, and Trajan succeeded him without difficulty. After an inspection tour along the Rhine and Danube frontiers, he returned to Rome and announced that he intended to be beneficent. And he was beneficent! Not just at first, but throughout his reign. He treated the Senate respectfully; built roads, aqueducts, and harbors in Italy; he even told provincial governors not to enforce the anti-Christian laws very strictly. In Rome, he put up some more buildings and spent enough on gladiatorial games and the like to ensure his popularity with the common people.

Certain foreigners, on the other hand, may not have liked Trajan so much, seeing as how he conquered them. First there were the Dacians, an aggressive people living north of the Danube who had fought the Romans to a draw in the days of Domitian. To Trajan, a draw against unruly barbarians was a blot on Rome's record, a blot that he decided to erase; it's possible, though unlikely, that he was also inspired by foreknowledge of the fact that Dacia was destined to be named Romania later on. The Dacians fought hard, but Trajan eventually triumphed, to the delight of the modern Romanians, since they would hate to be Slavs or Hungarians.

Meanwhile, in the east, Trajan had told a general of his to annex the Arabian client state centered around the city of Petra. (The so-called treasury building at Petra, actually a giant tomb carved out of solid rock, may look familiar to you, because it showed up in the third Indiana Jones movie). The Arabs didn't seem to mind being annexed very much. Their main interest was in cross-desert trade, and trade continued to flourish under Roman rule.

The "Treasury" at Petra

The Man Who Wouldn't Be King

Nerva, who appointed himself consul for 97, chose as his colleague Lucius Verginius Rufus. Rufus had been an army commander along the Rhine in the year 68 whose troops tried, unsuccessfully, to persuade him to declare himself emperor. In 69, he was in Rome when Otho committed suicide, and again some soldiers tried to make him announce his candidacy for the throne. This time, the soldiers were prepared to kill him if he refused, but he escaped by sneaking out the back door of his house when they weren't looking. His prudent conduct ensured that he lived to see the collapse of the Julio-Claudian, Galban, Othonian, Vitellian, and Flavian dynasties, and to die, later in 97, a man respected by all his compatriots.

Also in the east, the Parthians were making trouble in Armenia again by replacing the Roman-approved king with a different candidate. Trajan apparently decided that this Armenia-Parthia thing had been going on long enough. Therefore, in 114, he personally led a big army into Armenia and announced its annexation. It was all so easy that he decided to go ahead and conquer Parthia too, or at least the western parts of Parthia. The Parthians didn't put up much of a fight, and by 116, Trajan had marched all the way to the Persian Gulf, annexing as he went. But meanwhile the many Jews living in the eastern Mediterranean provinces, who were always at odds with the Greek inhabitants of the same region, had gone into open revolt against Rome. Then, in late 116, the newly conquered parts of Parthia rebelled. Trajan tried to suppress all the revolts, but doing so was kind of tiring, and he died in 117.

Trajan had no children. On his deathbed he adopted his lieutenant general and nearest adult male relative, Publius Aelius Hadrianus. At least Hadrian said he'd been adopted, and since the army accepted him, the Senate and people did too. Hadrian decided that Armenia and Parthia weren't worth the trouble it would take to keep them, but he did suppress the Jewish revolt. For a while, anyway. (Ooh, foreshadowing).

The Romans were never quite sure what to make of Hadrian (modern historians, who've never even met the man, are similarly perplexed). His reign got off to a bad start when the praetorian prefect arranged for the execution of four leading senators on vague charges of conspiracy. Hadrian, who hadn't been in Rome at the time, tried to deny responsibility for the executions, but the Senate never trusted him after that. The senators also weren't too pleased by the fact that Hadrian turned out to be a Greek-loving (ha-ha! [see box at right]) intellectual who liked Athens better than Rome and who spent more time touring the provinces or hanging out at his palatial country estate than he did in the capital city.

On the other hand, Hadrian's provincial tours, which lasted for several years at a time, had the serious purpose of letting him personally inspect the empire, improve local administration, and, above all, strengthen the defenses of the imperial frontier. For, unlike his predecessor, Hadrian thought that wars of conquest were unnecessary and overly expensive. Therefore, instead of invading people, he concentrated on improving the training and discipline of the troops stationed along the borders, and also built fortifications like the famous Hadrian's Wall in northern Britain. Many modern historians think that this policy of consolidation was wise, although it obviously contrasted ingloriously with Trajan's revival of the grand old tradition of conquering the neighbors.

Back in Italy, Hadrian updated the Roman code of law, put up lots of new buildings (including a refurbished Pantheon), and created new government programs to try to alleviate poverty. All of this activity, along with Hadrian's frequent absences from Rome, involved an expansion of the imperial

---

Death in ~~Venice~~ Egypt

Hadrian not only loved Greeks in general, he loved one Greek in particular, a handsome young fellow from Asia Minor named Antinous. Okay, maybe the middle-aged emperor's liking for the well-coiffed teenager was just a natural fatherly affection—and maybe Socrates didn't have any ulterior motives when he went on that walk in the country with Phaedrus. Whatever the nature of the affection, Hadrian was devastated when Antinous drowned in Egypt in the year 130.

Perhaps not surprisingly, Hadrian didn't get along with his wife, whom he'd married because she was Trajan's grandniece. They never had any children.

bureaucracy, which may or may not strike you as a good thing, depending on whether you vote Libertarian or Socialist in modern elections.

Hadrian's stupidest move was deciding, in the year 130, to put a new Greco-Roman city on the site of Jerusalem, which had been more or less in ruins ever since Titus captured it sixty years earlier. Worse yet, he planned to put a Roman temple on the site of the destroyed Jewish temple. Oops! It didn't take long for the Jews still living in Judea to start a revolt and seize control of most of the province. The rebellion wasn't crushed until 135, with great loss of life on both sides, especially among the Jews. Jews were thereafter forbidden to live in Judea, but the Jewish communities in other provinces went on as before.

By the time the mess he'd created in Judea was settled, Hadrian was old, sick, and crotchety. Sensing death approaching, and having no children, he eventually adopted a middle-aged senator named Titus Aurelius Antoninus. He also told Antoninus, who had no sons of his own, to adopt a couple of youngsters who were destined to succeed him; the elder of these youths had his name changed to Marcus Aurelius and married Antoninus' daughter. Then Hadrian, now very unpopular because he'd gotten so crotchety, died in the year 138. There was much rejoicing.

Antoninus, who earned the nickname Pius, or "Devoted," by treating his adoptive father's memory with reverence, ended up reigning until 161, a lot longer than anyone had expected. Not to worry, though, because just about everyone liked him. Unlike

Hadrian, he spent all his time in Rome and let his competent subordinates deal with the provinces. He cut taxes and government spending, though he increased spending on welfare for poor people; he also modified laws which bore harshly on the lower classes. There were a few minor foreign wars and a few unsuccessful rebellions during his reign, but for the most part, Rome was peaceful, prosperous, and well-governed during Antoninus' twenty-three years on the throne. Too bad there's nothing more to say about Antoninus, but since nothing really exciting happened during his reign, I guess we'll just move on to Marcus Aurelius.

Victorious Roman Soldiers, Returning from the East, Start to Realize that They Don't Feel So Good

Marcus assumed the throne with no difficulty on Antoninus Pius' death. Although he shared the imperial title for the first eight years of his reign with his adoptive younger brother, Lucius Verus, Marcus was plainly the one in charge. A good thing, too, since Lucius was lazy and spendthrift, but at least he had the good grace to die in 169, so that we don't have to say anything else about him. Meanwhile, Rome had gotten into yet another war with Parthia. See if you can guess what the name of the kingdom they were squabbling over this time (hint: the first five letters are A-r-m-e-n). The Romans, led by a capable general named Avidius Cassius, eventually won the war, but then the troops who came back to Rome for their victory parade brought some sort of eastern disease with them, and an epidemic resulted.

The epidemic's timing couldn't have been worse, because just then, in the late 160's, the Germans living north of the Danube decided to attack the empire. With Rome's manpower depleted by the plague, the Germans even crossed over the Alps into northern Italy, reminding people of the Cimbri and Teutones centuries before. Poor Marcus, a studious fellow who would much rather have stayed in Rome reading philosophy, had to take the field himself, along with whatever reinforcements he could scrounge up. It took a few years to drive the Germans back north of the Danube, whereupon Marcus decided that he might as well subdue them for good by conquering their homeland and adding it to the empire. This took a few more years, of course, but by 175 the enemy seemed ready to submit.

Alas, 175 was the year when, back in Syria, Avidius Cassius decided to declare himself emperor, apparently after hearing a rumor that Marcus was dead. Marcus made a compromise peace with the Germans and set out to fight the rebellious easterners. But before he could get there, some of Avidius' men, dismayed to learn that Marcus was alive after all, killed their leader and sent his head to Marcus, though not on a silver platter. Nevertheless, the damage was done. It took Marcus a couple of years to get back to trying to conquer the Germans, and he hadn't quite finished the task when he died in 180, leaving the throne to his eighteen-year-old son Commodus.

Welcome to the Roman Empire—A Nice Place to Live

According to Edward Gibbon, a long-armed Asian ape of the genus *Hylobates* who overcame his humble background to become one of England's greatest historians, "If a man were called to fix the period in the history of the world during which the condition of the human race was most happy and prosperous, he would, without hesitation, name that which elapsed from the death of Domitian to the accession of Commodus." Of course, now we have video games, but Gibbon didn't, and if we limit ourselves to video game-deprived societies, 2nd-century Rome certainly ranks pretty high. Wars under the five good emperors were mostly confined to the frontiers, rich people reaped the benefits of peace and good government, the poor were supported by government welfare programs, and even slaves and Christians weren't treated as badly as in the past. True, Marcus Aurelius' reign was marked by a foreign invasions and a devastating plague, but he did a good job of responding to the crises and keeping the empire intact. So he gets to be called a good emperor even though his times were troubled.

All of the good emperors, in fact, were conscientious rulers who took their job seriously and tried to rule both honorably and effectively. They didn't execute senators much, but on the other hand, they decreased the Senate's role in government by building up a civil service staffed by equites and answerable only to the emperor. Most senators didn't mind, though; there were still plenty of jobs available for ambitious senators, while unambitious senators enjoyed high social status without having to do any work. The Senate as a whole remained prestigious because, with most of the old republican aristocratic families having died off, its new members included the wealthiest and most influential men from Italy and the provinces.

Of course, there were problems under the five good emperors just like under any government—inflation, unemployment, the fact that beards came back into style—but on the whole, people were better off than they'd been, say, back when Romans and Carthaginians were killing each other all the time. And they were certainly better off than they were destined to be in the next chapter.

More Art and Literature (What is This, Humanities 101?)

It's often stated that Latin literature declined in quality after the reign of Augustus, but if you've ever read the works of the historian Tacitus, you may not be so sure. Plus, there were plenty of other writers both before and after Tacitus, so let's go through a list of some of the most prominent ones.

Seneca: Playwright and philosopher. We met him when he was helping Nero run things, before Nero sentenced him to death. His plays were very popular and influential during the Renaissance but are out of style now.

Petronius: Also lived in Nero's day, wrote a novel called the *Satyricon* in which he made fun of nouveau-riche people. Nero sentenced him to death, too.

Lucan: Seneca's nephew. Wrote a long, somewhat tedious epic poem about the civil war between Caesar and Pompey, in which Caesar was the bad guy. Do you think that Nero, who was Caesar's heir, sentenced Lucan to death? If you need more than one guess, you haven't been paying very close attention.

Pliny the Elder: Government official and man of science who was killed when he went to Pompeii to get a good look at the eruption of Mt. Vesuvius. Wrote an encyclopedia of sorts called *Natural History.*

Quintilian: Late 1st century professor of rhetoric. His book on the subject was very widely read for a long time, but who studies rhetoric nowadays?

Martial: Late 1st century author of short poems that the Romans found very amusing. I don't find them that amusing, but then, I'm not a Roman.

Pliny the Younger: Nephew of Pliny the Elder, avoided dying at Pompeii because he was too busy doing his homework to accompany his uncle on the fateful trip. Went on to become a leading government official during Trajan's day, as well as a writer of famous letters on a variety of topics.

Tacitus: Senator in late 1st-early 2nd century, outstanding stylist, wrote history, biography, and ethnography. Most famous for his history of the Julio-Claudian period. Having suffered through Domitian's reign, he wasn't particularly partial toward the imperial system of government, but he thought Trajan was okay.

Juvenal: Wrote satirical poems criticizing everyone and everything in Roman society. Even more bitter and pessimistic than Tacitus. Unlike Tacitus, he didn't think that things were any better under Trajan than they'd been previously.

Suetonius: Served as Hadrian's private secretary for a while. Author of gossipy, not always reliable, but consistently entertaining *Lives of the Twelve Caesars*, starting with Julius Caesar and ending with Domitian.

Apuleius: 2nd century novelist. His book *The Golden Ass* told the story of a man who turned into a donkey, then had various adventures. (Note to self: this would make a good plot for a TV sitcom). In Apuleius' book, the goddess Isis eventually turned the hero back into a man again.

Aulus Gellius: 2nd century essayist. Wrote a collection of essays called *Attic Nights*, not because he slept on the top floor of his house, but because Attica is the part of Greece where Athens is located, and Gellius was living in Athens when he started writing the book.

Speaking of Athens, I should mention that under the empire, there were all sorts of Roman citizens who wrote stuff in Greek, either because they happened to be Greeks, or because they thought Greek was more high-class than Latin. Even Marcus Aurelius recorded his personal philosophical musings in Greek. I won't go through all the Greco-Roman writers here (nor will I say anything at all about Greco-Roman wrestling), but I will mention two writers who are important as sources for Roman history.

Plutarch: Late 1st-early 2nd century biographer and essayist. His short biographies of famous Greeks and Romans are wonderful reading. Not as wonderful to read as Plutarch, but informative.

Appian: 2nd century author of a book on Roman military history.

The authors named above came from all over the empire—some from Rome, more of them from various provinces. In the late Republic, Roman authors had mostly been Italians born and bred. Likewise, republican politicians, and Augustus afterward, had mostly concentrated on putting fancy art and architecture in Italy, particularly in Rome; provinces, to a lot of Romans, were just there to be plundered. However, the provinces recovered economically under the emperors, and soon cities all over the place were putting up temples, amphitheaters, statues, and the like. In other words, Italy may have flourished culturally under Augustus, but later on, internal peace and prosperity led to a cultural efflorescence throughout the empire as whole. Which was a good thing.

Very Difficult Questions for Chapter Seven

no answers provided, lest you be tempted to cheat by looking at the answers right away
without first trying to figure out the correct answers yourself

The questions below are based on the portraits below, which depict three of the five good emperors. Except Question 5, which is based not on the portraits, but on Questions 1-3, but since Questions 1-3 are based on the portraits, I guess Question 5 could sort of be considered to be indirectly based on the portraits. Maybe.

1. Which two of the five good emperors are not depicted at left, mostly because they're not as famous as the other guys, one of them because he only reigned for about sixteen months, and so mostly served as a placeholder between Domitian and Trajan, and the other of them because, even though he reigned for a couple of decades, his reign was peaceful and pleasant, and therefore rather dull?

2. Which of the emperors depicted at left didn't have a beard, but did have a rather silly-looking haircut, yet nevertheless overcame his silly hairstyle to become an excellent general and one of Rome's best emperors before dying in the year 117 AD?

3. Which one of the four emperors is shown at left riding a horse, just like in a famous statue of him that you can still see in Rome, or, if you don't want to pay the entrance fee for the museum, just like in a replica of the statue that you can see for free on top of the Capitoline Hill, which is where the original statue stood from 1528, which is when Michelangelo had it moved there from somewhere else, until it was moved inside in the mid-twentieth century, but they put a replica where the original had stood?

4. Which of the emperors depicted at left has not been asked about yet?

5. Why are the sentences in Questions 1-3 so long? Were they originally written in German or something?

Trajan

Hadrian

Marcus Aurelius

Pugilistic Interlude

Welcome to London, England, in the year 1787, where our featured event is a bare-knuckle bout between "Fat" Eddie Gibbon and Tom "Giver of" Paine. We join the action in the third round.

PAINE: *(tagging Gibbon with a couple of quick jabs)* Liberty, sir! Where, under your "good" emperors, was liberty?

GIBBON: *(landing a short left hook to Paine's midsection)* Liberty doesn't feed the poor. The good emperors fed them.

PAINE: *(bobbing and weaving, flitting jabs toward the advancing foe)* So too does the farmer set his sheep to graze, the better to fleece them.

GIBBON: *(trying to slide his counterpunches past Paine's defenses)* And the farmer protects the sheep from wolves. Both sides benefit.

PAINE: *(resting on the ropes for a minute while warding off Gibbon's blows)* Sir, you ignore a crucial point…

GIBBON: *(throwing a right cross which Paine avoids)* What's that?

PAINE: *(staggering Gibbon with an overhand right)* Men are not sheep!

GIBBON: *(backpedaling, trying to clear his head)* It was your metaphor to begin with. I suppose you prefer the Republic.

PAINE: *(throwing a flurry of punches)* Indeed, for republics are built on virtue! The self-reliant Romans of the Republic cared about the nation, for they had a stake in its government. It was republican Rome which conquered the world, imperial Rome which lost it.

GIBBON: *(steadier on his feet now)* Not till imperial Rome became Christian and lost its manly virtue. It was the Christian church, not monarchy, that destroyed Rome in the end.

PAINE: *(pausing)* Oh. Actually, I agree with you about the Christian church being a bad thing. I'm a deist myself.

GIBBON: *(straightening up)* Really? Then what are we fighting about?

The crowd, confused and annoyed by the abrupt halt in the proceedings, begins to boo and throw things at the erstwhile combatants.

PAINE: *(to the crowd)* Hear me, good people! If it is freedom and contentment that you wish, you must first throw off the shackles of the established Christian chu—

Suddenly Paine falls to the ground, having just been thwocked on the head by a mighty blow from the club-wielding James "The Drunken Scotsman" Boswell, who has burst through the crowd and into the ring.

BOSWELL: Shtinkin' atheist! *(turns toward Gibbon)* And that goes for you, too! *(waves his club menacingly)*

Gibbon, terrified, tries to flee, but the spectators, like all working class spectators at 19th-century boxing matches in England, are good honest Church of England men, always ready to pummel dissenters if the opportunity should arise. We have to cut to commercial before seeing the denouement, but there seems to be little doubt that Gibbon, like Paine, is destined to end the day in the hospital.

THE HISTORY OF ROME

Chapter Eight

*in which things fall apart, the center cannot hold,
and mere anarchy is loosed upon the world*

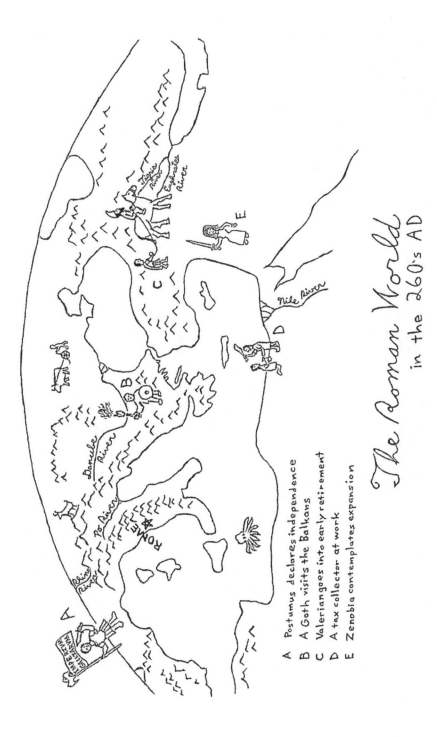

A Postumus declares independence
B A Goth visits the Balkans
C Valerian goes into early retirement
D A tax collector at work
E Zenobia contemplates expansion

The Roman World
in the 260's AD

Hercules, Hannibal, and Alexander the Great

Things weren't looking especially cheery upon the accession of Emperor Commodus in 180 AD. Hostile barbarians, declining population, lack of civic spirit, top-heavy bureaucracy, high taxes, inflation, unemployment, European technopop—okay, that last one hadn't been invented yet, but it's so bad that it makes the list anyway.

Commodus (who, in case you've forgotten, was Marcus Aurelius' eighteen-year-old son) decided that the best way to deal with all these problems was to forget about conquering the Germans and go back to Rome so he could fight as a gladiator in the Colosseum. No, I'm not kidding. Luckily, the Germans had been so soundly thrashed recently that they kept pretty quiet for the next thirty years. Back in the empire, though, the rich oppressed the poor, bandits roamed the countryside, and Commodus gradually went nuts. (He eventually came to believe that he was the god Hercules, who, like Commodus, was big, dumb, and liked to fight). Naturally, there were plots against the incompetent megalomaniac, but none succeeded until Dec. 31, 192, when the emperor's closest associates, who were embarrassed by his nuttiness, arranged to have him strangled.

It's a good thing that Commodus was killed on Dec. 31 instead of Jan. 1, because otherwise 193, like 69, would be called The Year of Four Emperors, and that would be confusing. Instead, it's just a year with three emperors, which apparently isn't enough to demand capitalization. The first of the three emperors was a well-respected general and senator named Pertinax, whom Commodus' ministers nominated and the Senate gladly confirmed. Alas, poor Pertinax, he annoyed the Praetorian Guard by trying to restore the military discipline that had fallen apart under Commodus. Not much caring for discipline, the praetorians mutinied, killed Pertinax, and handed the throne over to a wealthy senator named Didius Julianus, who had won their support by promising to give them a large cash payout.

Commodus, Dressed Up as Hercules
(note the lion skin and club)

As usual, the unarmed Senate ratified the heavily-armed praetorians' decision. However, the frontier legions didn't see why they shouldn't try to get their own favorite sons into office instead. Within a month, there were two new claimants to the throne, supported by the Danubian legions and the eastern legions, respectively. The Danubian commander, Septimius Severus, quickly marched his armies into Italy, where the praetorians, who enjoyed intimidating the Senate but weren't so eager to fight against other real-live soldiers, took the easy way out and murdered Didius.

Thus Septimius Severus became the third emperor of the year 193—the guy out east doesn't count, because the Senate never ratified his claim. Unfortunately, the eastern claimant wasn't willing to back down, plus the commanding general in Britain also had imperial ambitions. Civil war ensued, and it wasn't till 197 that Severus had conquered both his eastern and his western rivals.

If Commodus was Hercules, then maybe Severus was Hannibal. Not only was he born in Africa of Punic ancestry, but he seemed to share Hannibal's lack of high regard for the people of Italy. The Praetorian Guard, for example, was traditionally made up mostly of Italians, but they hadn't wowed Severus with their sterling conduct over the past few years. So he disbanded the whole unit and replaced it with a new, bigger Praetorian Guard composed of soldiers from all over the empire. He also promoted so many provincials to the Senate that Italians became a minority there. Not that being a senator was such an important job as it had once been, inasmuch as Severus mostly relied on the imperial bureaucracy to run things.

So old Double-S (which is a nickname that I just invented, and I plan to copyright it in case Septimius Severus comes back to life someday, because I think he'll think it's cool and maybe will pay me a lot of money for the rights to use it) wasn't too popular with the old-line senatorial nobility. But he was plenty popular with the troops, to whom he had given increased pay and privileges. A good thing, too, because Double-S (you'll get used to the nickname after a while) needed loyal soldiers for his campaigns in the east and in Britain, where foreign peoples had taken advantage of the civil war to cause trouble.

The Parthians were the biggest threat, so Double-S (actually, the nickname's starting to annoy me) spent several years campaigning against them and, when he was done, had actually converted the northern part of modern-day Iraq into a new province called Mesopotamia—the first time since Trajan that someone had added a whole new province to the empire. Way to go, Double-S! (Okay, I admit it, the nickname was a bad idea. I'll stop now.) He seems to have wanted to conquer northern Britain as well, but after a few years campaigning there, he

died in 211, after a reign of almost twenty years.

Some years before his death, Severus had built an arch in the Roman Forum, an arch which is still standing today. I'd be willing to bet that every single day of the year, tourists who've heard of emperors like Augustus, Nero, and Marcus Aurelius look at the arch and say, "Who the hell was Septimius Severus?" That's too bad, because Severus was actually a pretty successful emperor who deserves a lot of credit for stabilizing the tottering imperial system. He not only chastened Rome's foreign enemies, he also accumulated a treasury surplus, initiated much-needed reforms in the legal system, and encouraged a minor intellectual renaissance sponsored by his wife, a Syrian woman named Julia Domna. But on the down side, he raised taxes, killed lots of Christians and senators, and made it clear to everyone, including the soldiers themselves, that his position depended entirely upon the support of the armies. That was okay so long as there was an emperor, like Severus, who had unanimous backing from the troops, but it was destined to cause trouble in future years.

For now, though, the armies, having been loyal to Severus, were equally loyal to his sons Caracalla and Geta, who became co-emperors after Severus' death. Too bad the boys hated each other. Despite their mom's plea that they try to get along, it took less than a year for Caracalla, at age twenty-two the elder of the two, to have Geta assassinated. Then Caracalla left Rome and went to fight the Germans who, thirty years after Marcus Aurelius' death, were finally feeling frisky enough to threaten the frontier again. Luckily, Caracalla, like his dad, was a tough-guy soldier type, and he defeated the Germans pretty quickly.

But Caracalla was sure that he had a higher destiny than killing Germans. To wit, he hoped to do what no earlier Roman leader had ever done by conquering the whole Parthian Empire. In his own mind, that would make him the equal of Alexander the Great, the most famous general of ancient times. Just in case anyone missed the point, he even trained sixteen thousand Macedonians to fight like Alexander's phalanx, with long spears instead of the sword of the Roman legionary. However, tough guy or not, Caracalla wasn't much of a strategist. When he marched into Parthian territory in 216, the Parthian army just melted away into the mountains, leaving him no one to fight. Stymied, Caracalla marched back to Roman territory for the winter, where he was assassinated in early 217 by his praetorian prefect, Macrinus, who was accompanying the boss on the eastern expedition.

Why did Macrinus kill Caracalla? Maybe I should have mentioned earlier that Caracalla was a pretty lousy emperor, despotic, spendthrift, and given to executing people on the merest suspicion of disloyalty. Not just potentially rebellious senators and generals, either; for example, he personally supervised a massacre of the general populace of Alexandria, Egypt, because some of them had made disparaging comments about tyrants who murdered their own kid brothers. And of course, he killed lots of Christians all over the empire, on the theory that all Christians were disloyal.

Still, Caracalla's reign wasn't a complete disaster domestically, because the emperor himself usually paid little attention to non-military affairs, thus leaving things in the hands of his competent and cultured mother Julia Domna. However, the increased pay that the emperor lavished on his soldiers helped drive the state to bankruptcy, leading to increased taxation, currency devaluation, and attendant economic problems. Lack of revenue was also probably key to the decision, in 212, to proclaim that all free inhabitants of the empire were now full Roman citizens, a change which made them all liable to pay the inheritance tax that, by a remarkable coincidence, just happened to get doubled at exactly the same time.

Nevertheless, the proclamation was the culmination of an important social development, a natural follow-up to Severus' policy of treating provincials as equals, rather than subjects of an empire run by and for the people of Italy. Not that the people of the provinces were free of subjecthood, since now everyone was a subject of the emperor.

None of this mattered much to Macrinus, of course. What mattered to him was that, from inspecting the emperor's correspondence, he came to believe that he was going to be executed soon on suspicion of disloyalty. So he acted first, killed Caracalla, told the troops that Caracalla (whom the troops liked even if nobody else did) had died of natural causes, and then got the army to name him the new emperor. As always, the Senate, hearing what the soldiers wanted, said, "Okey-doke."

So I Sing a Song of Love, Julia

Julia Domna committed suicide after hearing of Caracalla's death, thus apparently bringing the Severan dynasty to a definitive end. Not so fast! Macrinus lost the respect of his gung-ho soldiers by making peace with the Parthians instead of conquering them. Then he announced plans to cut the army's pay back to what it had been before Caracalla's reign. Julia Domna's wealthy and ambitious sister, Julia Maesa, saw her opportunity. Maesa had two daughters, Julia Soaemias and Julia Mamaea, each of whom had a single son. In early 218, Grandma started spreading the rumor that Soaemias' fourteen-year-old son Elagabalus was actually Caracalla's illegitimate offspring—evidently Soaemias didn't mind being charged with having had an adulterous affair with her own cousin. The army, loyal to the Severan dynasty and unhappy with Macrinus, swung Elagabalus' way, and Macrinus was put to death.

So now Elagabalus, the hereditary priest of a local Syrian sun-god, was officially in charge of the whole Roman Empire. However, when he showed up in Rome in early 219, it turned out that the teenage emperor had zero interest in affairs of state. Rather, he devoted himself to three main activities: (1) promoting the worship of his foreign god, (2) acquiring fabulously expensive clothing, jewelry, and home furnishings, and (3) sharing his bed with a variety of big strong men. Meanwhile, his mother gave jobs and money to unqualified personal favorites and executed people who objected to the new regime. Julia Maesa soon realized that the soldiers were none too pleased with their outlandish emperor. To avoid being killed herself in the brewing army mutiny, she got Elagabalus to adopt his younger cousin Alexander, Julia Mamaea's son. Then Maesa and Mamaea arranged to have Elagabalus and Soaemias killed by the Praetorian Guard in 222. Nice family, those Severans. I'd wouldn't want to be related to them.

Alexander (who, like Elagabalus, became emperor at age fourteen) added the name Severus to his own when he succeeded to the throne, but he didn't share his family's violent tendencies. On the contrary, he was a nice boy who, even after he grew up, always did what his mother told him—also what his grandmother told him, but she died soon after his accession. Mamaea did a pretty good job running things for her son: she appointed competent officials, was polite to the Senate, cut expenditures, and lowered taxes when possible. She also abandoned the policy of torturing Christians to death, and saw no reason to initiate costly foreign wars.

Unfortunately, after several years of peace, some foreigners decided to initiate a war themselves. These foreigners were the Persians, who, unbeknownst to many a Roman, had been hanging around in southwestern Iran for hundreds of years,

waiting for a chance to overthrow the Parthians and retake their old position as rulers of all the Iranian peoples. They did just that in the 220's, and then decided that they ought to conquer the whole Middle East as well, since that's what the old-timey Persians had done. They started by invading the Roman province of Mesopotamia, in the year 230, thus forcing Mamaea and her son to bring extra troops out from Europe to fight them off. The removal of large numbers of troops from Europe, however, caused the Germans to get rambunctious again, so in 233 the emperor and his mommy hurried back to Europe. After some desultory fighting in 234, they decided, in 235, that paying the Germans to behave was safer than attacking them. Unfortunately for Alexander and mom, the Roman soldiers were outraged by their rulers' pusillanimity; moreover, they thought that if there was any extra cash lying around they, not the Germans, ought to get it. So they rebelled, killed Alexander Severus and Julia Mamaea, and put a leading general on the throne. This time, the Severan dynasty really had come to a definitive end.

Sublimely Ridiculous

The next several decades of Roman history can be seen as tragedy or as farce—tragedy if you had to live through them, farce if you're viewing them from the safety of many centuries' distance. Lucky for us we're in the latter category.

Before going into the amusing details of what actually happened, though, perhaps it behooves us to try to see exactly why things fell apart the way they did in the 3rd century. Or maybe it doesn't behoove us, but we're going to do so anyway, because announcing that we were going to do so gave me an excuse to use the word "behoove" in a sentence, which makes me happy because it's not a word that one gets to use much nowadays.

Starting with things that were beyond anyone's control, we find frequent epidemics and hostile foreigners. Of the latter, the Persians were much more aggressive than the Parthians had ever been, while the Germans and other northern barbarians were positively rampageous (I just made that word up, but I think it's a good one). Plagues and foreign invasions helped to bring about civic disorder, economic weakness, fiscal problems, tax increases, and a generally unhappy civilian population.

The soldiers, on the other hand, were riding high. They had figured out that they could be unruly without being punished too severely, since the emperors needed their support. Indeed, they could even nominate new emperors whenever they wanted, in hopes of getting a nice cash gift in return. Unfortunately, since the soldiers didn't always agree on who should be emperor, civil wars resulted. But the civil wars usually weren't too bloody, because one side or the other would chicken out and murder its emperor rather than risk a battle.

As for the emperors themselves, they had to worry not just about being killed by foreign enemies or their own troops, but also about conspiracies or outright revolts led by wealthy senators, ambitious governors, successful generals, or the emperors' own top lieutenants. In fact, some historians think that all but one of the many emperors who reigned between 235 and 285 died a violent death, the one certain exception being a guy who died of plague after ruling less than two years. Despite this abysmal record, there was never any shortage of would-be usurpers, with the result that fighting off foreigners or trying to govern the country efficiently frequently took a back seat to the fun of competing for the throne.

Without effective control from the top, lower-ranking officials became lazy and

---

Like Elagabalus, the Currency is Debased

The Roman emperors didn't print paper money; instead, they minted gold and silver coins (and modestly put their own pictures on them). Nor did they have the concept of deficit spending. So when the government was short on funds, as was often the case in these days of economic weakness and heavy military expenditure, it could only keep producing money to pay its debts by decreasing the amount of gold or silver in each coin. Naturally, people noticed that the coins had less valuable metal in them than in the old days, so they started charging more for the same goods and services. Voilà, inflation! Not good for the economy, as Jimmy Carter learned to his chagrin, but hard to put a stop to once it's started.

---

corrupt. Meanwhile, wealthy landowners and unscrupulous military men oppressed and robbed small farmers and townsfolk without fear of official reprisal. The middle class shrank, and poor people launched feeble revolts or turned to banditry. In other words, 3rd century Rome had become…a banana republic. (Except that it wasn't a republic, and it didn't have any bananas).

Now let's briefly run through the most important political-military events of this rather lunatic period. The general who replaced Alexander Severus in 235 was named Maximinus the Thracian (I call him Max Thrax for short). He fought the Germans successfully, doubled the army's pay, raised taxes on everyone else, and ignored the Senate. In 238, some people in Africa, upset by high taxes, rebelled and named their governor and his son emperors as Gordian I and II. The Senate, upset about being ignored, confirmed the Gordians' claim, but then a general loyal to Max Thrax killed Gordian I and II both. So the Senate chose two men from its own ranks, Pupienus and Balbinus, to be co-emperors. Max Thrax marched into Italy to fight them, but his troops mutinied and killed him. Then the Praetorian Guard mutinied against Pupienus and Balbinus, killed them, and named Gordian I's thirteen-year-old grandson emperor as Gordian III. Thus 238 became a year of six emperors.

A few years later, the Persians invaded Mesopotamia again, so Gordian went east with some extra troops and generals and drove them out again. Meanwhile, northern barbarians harassed the Danubian provinces. Then, in 244, a general named Philip the Arab killed Gordian and named himself emperor. He made peace with the Persians and went back to Rome, where he celebrated the city's 1000th birthday in 247 (like most people, Philip believed Livy's claim that Rome had been founded in 753 BC). He also survived several armed rebellions, but then in 249 a Danubian general named Decius claimed the throne, marched into Italy, and killed Philip.

Decius' departure from the frontier had permitted a Germanic tribe called the Goths to rampage across the Danube. Decius was less interested in fighting than in restarting Rome's dormant Christian-killing policy, but eventually he went back to oppose the Goths. Surprise! The Goths defeated and killed him in 251. The remnants of Decius' forces immediately chose Decius' lieutenant Trebonianus Gallus as the new emperor. Gallus, having determined that Rome would be a nicer place to live than the barbarian-infested Balkans, heroically abandoned his army and headed for the capital, leaving the Goths mostly free to loot and pillage. "We'll loot," decided some of the more administratively-minded Goths, "you guys pillage, and you guys over there can just plain plunder." Meanwhile, the Persians invaded Mesopotamia and Syria, and a devastating plague spread throughout the empire.

In 253, the troops who'd been abandoned in the Balkans proclaimed their commander Aemilian as emperor, then marched into Italy ("Let's get the hell out of the Goth-infested Balkans," that was their motto). In Italy, Gallus' outnumbered troops quickly killed their emperor, but then the commander of the Rhine army, Valerian, appeared with his own army and a corresponding claim to the throne.

Aemilian's men quickly assassinated Aemilian, and suddenly Valerian was the emperor of those parts of the Roman world that hadn't been overrun by foreigners or fallen under the control of local warlords.

At least Valerian, unlike Gallus, tried to do something to restore the empire. Leaving his son Gallienus in charge in Europe, Valerian himself went to the east to fight the Persians. But Valerian was not a great general, plus he was scared (with good reason) that if he gave any of his subordinates too large an army, said subordinate would revolt against him. The upshot was that the Persians outfought him consistently. Eventually, in 260, they captured the emperor himself and subsequently overran eastern Asia Minor.

Gallienus, alas, couldn't do anything to stop the Persians—he had his hands full with barbarians and rebels in Europe. When Valerian had marched into Italy in 253, the Germans along the Rhine had sneaked into Gaul behind him, and some of them eventually made their way as far as northern Italy. Meanwhile, the Goths and various associated tribes swarmed into Greece and even into western Asia Minor. Gradually, Gallienus and his officers were able to push the barbarians back, but then the news of Valerian's capture prompted four (!) separate rebellions in late 260. Gallienus defeated all but one of the rebels, but the last, a general named Postumus, was able to set himself up as independent emperor in Gaul, Spain, and Britain.

A lesser man, like me, might have said, "The hell with this. I'm getting on a boat and sailing to China." Gallienus, in contrast, never lost hope; instead, he did what he could to stave off utter collapse over the next eight years. The Roman position in the east was restored through the efforts of the pro-Roman city of Palmyra in the Syrian desert, while Gallienus concentrated on fighting the Goths and forming a new elite cavalry corps to help him in future wars. But then in 268, while suppressing a revolt in northern Italy, he was assassinated by his own top officers, one of whom, Claudius, became the next emperor.

After a quick visit to Rome to say hi to the Senate, Claudius marched off to the Balkans, where a major victory over the Goths won him the nickname Gothicus. Then he died of plague in 270. His successor was his brother Quintillus, a nonentity who was quickly dethroned later in the year by a general named Aurelian.

Aurelian must have been an incurable optimist, if he was willing to take on the job of emperor in such circumstances. Postumus had been killed by his own insubordinate troops in 269, but the Gallic Empire remained independent. Claudius had quieted the Goths somewhat, but other Germans were still harassing Italy, and the Danubian provinces had been devastated. In the east, Palmyra had driven back the Persians, but now Palmyra's queen, Zenobia, was starting to take over all of Rome's eastern provinces for herself. Could this be the end of the Roman Empire? Probably not, since there are two more chapters left in the book. But if you want to know for sure, you'll have to go on to the next chapter.

A New Model Army

The Romans had always had their difficulties when fighting against Parthians and Germans. But as we've seen, thing got even worse in the 3rd century. How come?

The most obvious problem was that Rome's armies spent as much time fighting each other in civil wars as they spent fighting foreigners. But another important factor was that Rome's enemies had become more formidable. The Parthian Empire had been a loosely organized feudal state with a relatively unadventurous foreign policy. The Persian Empire, on the other hand, was a centralized monarchy with definite annexationist ambitions. Like the Parthians, the Persians had lots of cavalry that could outmaneuver Roman legionary infantry on open ground. Unlike the Parthians, they also had learned up-to-date techniques of siege warfare, so they could actually capture fortresses and major cities instead of just riding through the fields burning crops and so on.

As for the Germans, the Romans had previously been able to hold them at bay in part because they were grouped into lots of little tribes that individually weren't that threatening. Beginning in the late 2nd century, though, big new tribes like the Goths migrated to the borders, while smaller tribal units coalesced into larger and more aggressive confederations. The Germans weren't great at siege warfare, but they were fierce warriors and were expert at plundering defenseless villages.

More formidable enemies meant that, declining population notwithstanding, the Romans needed a bigger army; more legions, more auxiliaries, more everything. The legions were usually stationed on the frontiers and thus tended to become garrison troops, frequently recruited from the local population. But Rome also needed a central reserve force for times when invaders broke through the frontier defenses. The praetorians could serve that function to some degree, but there weren't enough of them, plus the Romans figured out that they needed more cavalry if they wanted to fight successfully against the Persians. Hence Gallienus' elite cavalry corps.

Cavalry, unfortunately, are expensive—and so, in general, are big armies that demand ever-higher pay and frequent cash gifts. No wonder taxes were so high.

Thought-Provoking Questions for Chapter Eight

1. Suppose Commodus was right, and he really was the reincarnation of Hercules (though that wouldn't explain how a mere mortal was able to strangle him to death). If reincarnation is possible, then maybe some of the emperors named in this chapter have been reincarnated in modern-day America. Assuming that's the case, match the emperor in the left-hand column with his reincarnation in the right-hand column.

    (a) Commodus   (x) Donald Trump
    (b) Didius Julianus   (y) Mike Tyson
    (c) Elagabalus   (z) Kim Kardashian

2. Which emperor or co-emperors from this chapter had the silliest name(s)?

    (a) Didius
    (b) Elagabalus
    (c) Pupienus & Balbinus

3. Which of the following is the coolest nickname?

    (a) Double-S
    (b) Max Thrax
    (c) Gothicus

4. Speaking of people subject to monarchs (which I was doing back on p. 88), did you know that Australians, unlike Americans, are still officially subjects of Queen Elizabeth of England, rather than free citizens of an independent republic?

Answers: 1. (a)=(y), (b)=(x), (c)=(z)
                 2. (c)
                 3. I'm partial to (b) myself, but some people might legitimately prefer (c). Definitely not (a).
                 4. I don't know if you knew about Australians' subjecthood or not. Regardless, you know now, and if you know any Australians, you could use your knowledge to taunt them sometime.
                     Note #1: Make sure you're standing at a safe distance before you commence the taunting. Some Australians are a little bit touchy about such matters.
                     Note #2: Canadians are also subjects of Queen Elizabeth, but they're actually rather proud of the fact, so you'll have to find something else to taunt them about.

Lexicographic Interlude

Goth (def. 1)

Goth (gɑθ), *noun*—**1.** A member of a Germanic tribe that played a prominent role in the fall of the Roman Empire, beginning in the 3rd century AD, and thus helped to usher in the Middle Ages. **2.** A modern-day young person who signals disaffection with mainstream culture by listening to gloomy music and by wearing black clothing and stark makeup.

Gothic (gɑθɪk), *adjective or noun*—**1.** Of or related to the ancient Goths or their language. **2.** Of or related to the Middle Ages. **3.** Of or related to the culture of northern Europe in the late Middle Ages, especially **(a)** Gothic script, a font characterized by heavy serifs, **(b)** Gothic architecture, characterized by tall churches with stained-glass windows and pointy arches, and **(c)** Gothic art, which tends to be more naturalistic and emotionally expressive than earlier medieval sculpture and painting. **4. (a)** A modern literary style emphasizing darkness, gloom, and mystery, which are often associated with the medieval world by modern people who think that ruined Gothic buildings are spooky; **(b)** by extension, anything or anyone dark and gloomy.

Goth (def. 2)

𝔓ater noster qui es in caelis

Gothic (def. 3(a))

American Gothic, *proper noun*—A 1930 painting by American artist Grant Wood that depicts two people standing in front of an 1880's house built in Gothic revival style, with a pointy roof and a pointed-arch window.

Gothic moth, *noun*—A European moth with patterns on its wings that resemble the patterns of interconnected structural supports on the ceiling of a typical medieval Gothic building.

American Gothic

Gothic (def. 3(b))

THE HISTORY OF ROME

Chapter Nine

in which, somehow or other, the Romans manage to put Humpty-Dumpty together again

and also in which Napoleon Bonaparte, who has been absent from this book since Chapter Two, makes an unexpected and not very apropos reappearance on the map below, on board a British ship that's taking him as a prisoner to the South Atlantic island of St. Helena

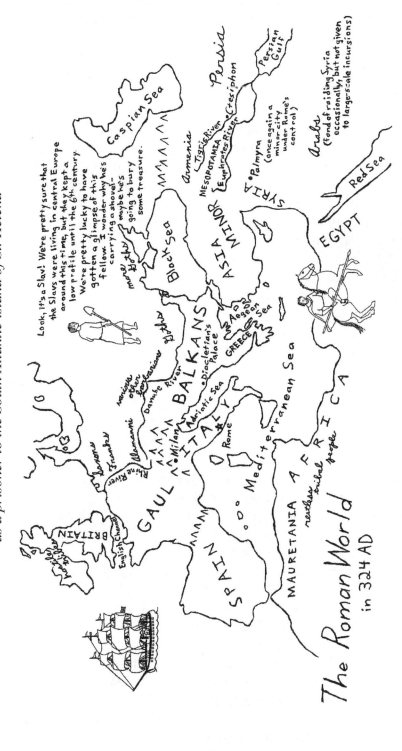

Look, it's a Slav! We're pretty sure that the Slavs were living in central Europe around this time, but they kept a low profile until the 6th century. We're pretty lucky to have gotten a glimpse of this fellow. I wonder why he's carrying a shovel — maybe he's going to bury some treasure.

The Roman World in 324 AD

The Apotheosis of Aurelian

Time: 275 AD

Place: the Deified Emperors' Lounge on Mt. Olympus. The lounge is a fairly dreary place, with dim, flickering fluorescent lights, dusty 1970's-era furniture, a lot of yellowish newspapers and old magazines lying around, and a small black-and-white TV in one corner.

Aurelian enters through the front door, carrying a battered old suitcase. He peers around in the gloom, and then addresses a disheveled old man sitting on a couch near the door, with piles of books and papers around him.

AURELIAN: Excuse me, can you tell me where I can find Claudius?

CLAUDIUS I: I'm C-c-c-claudius. Wh-who are you?

AURELIAN: No, I mean Claudius II, Gothicus. I'm his friend Aurelian.

CLAUDIUS II: *(hastening over from the other side of the room, where he had been playing checkers with Augustus)* Aurelian! Good to see you! Sorry it had to be so soon, though. I'd kind of hoped you might last a decade or so.

CLAUDIUS I: *(muttering to himself as he turns back to his books)* No one ever c-comes to see me.

AURELIAN: *(to Claudius II)* Yeah, I'd hoped so too. Funny thing is, the conspirators who killed me weren't even out to overthrow me, exactly—they were just some of my staff officers and household servants who thought I was going to execute them for corruption. *(pauses)* Oh, and speaking of overthrowing people, sorry about your brother.

CLAUDIUS II: Forget about it. He was a nonentity. I'm glad you took over. So anyway, come over here, I'd like you to meet some people. Hey, everybody, it's Aurelian, newly deified!

A few of the other middle-aged and elderly men in the room get up, but most pay no attention. The newcomers are Trajan, an elderly but still vigorous fellow with a piercing gaze; Antoninus Pius, a kindly-looking old man; and Augustus, who appears to be annoyed with Claudius for abandoning the checkers game so precipitately.

AURELIAN: *(recognizing the three dead emperors from their portrait busts)* Oh, wow, it's great to meet you guys. This is a real honor.

TRAJAN: So you're the one who abandoned Dacia! Do you know how much trouble it was for me to conquer it in the first place? Plus you gave up that little triangle of land in southwestern Germany.

AURELIAN: Wait a minute, they'd both already been overrun and effectively lost back in Gallienus' day. All I did was reposition the remaining troops and settlers from Dacia to the south of the Danube, where they helped stabilize the Balkans. Not to mention that I drove back the Germanic invaders of Italy, reconquered the east from the Palmyrenes, and also reconquered the secessionist Gallic Empire.

ANTONINUS: Of course, of course, you did lots of wonderful things. Don't be so hard on the boy, Trajan. Why, he even put a little bit of silver back in the currency, and he put up a nice new wall around Rome, just in case the barbarians come back to Italy someday.

AUGUSTUS: In my day, we didn't need walls around the city. The emperor kept Rome's enemies from crossing the frontiers.

CLAUDIUS II: Oh, I'm sick of hearing about your day. In your day, you didn't have half the problems we 3rd century emperors have had to face. Maybe if you'd conquered Germany instead of running away after you lost three legions, things would be easier nowadays.

AUGUSTUS: Oh, here we go again. Poor 3rd century emperors. Look, I built the empire; is it asking too much of you guys just to hold it together? *(turning to Aurelian)* And another thing, what's with this worship of the Unconquered Sun that you tried to make the official state religion? Jupiter and Mars aren't good enough for you?

AURELIAN: *(embarrassed to be arguing with Augustus, but unwilling to back down)* Look, I know things were different in the old days, but nobody takes that Jupiter and Mars stuff seriously anymore. Heck, seems like half the people in the Greek-speaking cities of the east are going in for that weird Christian sect. *(looking around)* I suppose that's why you're not getting enough donations from believers to keep this place up better.

ANTONINUS: Oh, it's not so bad, really. Sure, the budget's a little tight, but we've each got our own room, and the grounds are nice. Would you like to see the grounds?

AURELIAN: Okay, if you're not too busy. Mind if I put my stuff away first? The staff said my room would have my name on the door.

CLAUDIUS II: Sure, it should be right down the hall here. Come with me, I'll show you, then we can take a walk in the garden.

ANTONINUS: I'll wait for you guys here. *(to Augustus and Trajan)* Are you two coming with us?

AUGUSTUS: Nah, I'm gonna watch the games. Welcome to Elysium, Aurelian. *(He strolls over toward the TV, turns it on, and starts fiddling with the antenna)*.

TRAJAN: Yeah, why not. I'd like to hear more about these heavy cavalry tactics you guys have dreamed up. Claudius says you're the real expert on cavalry, Aurelian.

CLAUDIUS II: Great, we'll be back in five minutes.

Aurelian and Claudius II exit via a hallway, their voices fading in the distance. Trajan and Antoninus sit down to wait; almost immediately, the latter's eyes close and his head droops onto his chest. Soon, his snores make a pleasant accompaniment to Claudius I's muttering and the drone of the TV set, the only other sounds that disturb the quiet of the Deified Emperors' Lounge.

Diocletian Has a New Plan

Meanwhile, back on earth, no one had expected Aurelian's assassination, so it took a while (between a few weeks and several months—historians still argue about this, as if they had nothing better to do with their time) for the army and the Senate to agree on his successor. Whoever they chose would face a daunting task. Yes, Aurelian had reconquered both east and west, the Balkans were quieter than they'd been for a while, and the Persians, having been bested by the Palmyrenes in the 260's, didn't seem bent on conquering the whole Middle East anymore. On the other hand, Goths and other barbarians were still harassing Asia Minor; Gaul, after the collapse of the Gallic Empire, was disaffected and vulnerable to attacks by Germans living across the Rhine; tribal people in Africa, northern Britain, and elsewhere were restless; and citizens everywhere suffered from a weak economy, high taxes, and inefficient government. As in times past, desperate poor people turned to brigandage as a way out of their difficulties, which may have worked out okay for the brigands but didn't do much for civil order in general.

But the biggest problem may have been the army. On the one hand, the reforms under recent emperors had improved military efficiency. Not only had the heavy cavalry reserve proved its worth, but the military crisis had resulted in generalships being passed out not to inexperienced senators, but to professional soldiers, often risen from the ranks. Moreover, since the times demanded that an emperor be above all a good general, that meant that capable men of humble birth, like Claudius II and Aurelian, could succeed to the throne. On the other hand, it also meant that just about any general could aspire to the throne if he felt like it—and a lot of them felt like it. In addition, since emperors weren't from noble and respected families anymore, people felt less reverence for the imperial office than previously. (Aurelian's promotion of the Unconquered Sun, whose divine representative on earth he claimed to be, was at least partly an attempt to elevate his own status so that people would be less inclined to assassinate him. As we've seen, it didn't work.) And the troops, many of them barbarians whom the emperors recruited due to the shortage of citizen soldiers, were always eager for cash bonuses from a new emperor, and so were more ready than ever to support a usurper. Put it all together, and it's no surprise that there continued to be lots of military revolts, conspiracies, assassinations, and civil wars for the next couple of decades. As usual, the civil wars often weren't particularly sanguinary, since the troops on one side or another frequently killed their own emperor rather than fight an all-out battle. Still, even relatively non-sanguinary civil wars aren't much good for a country's welfare.

Problems notwithstanding, Rome needed an emperor, and in late 275, the army and the Senate agreed on one, a militarily experienced ex-consul named Tacitus (probably not related to the historian of the same name). As mentioned above, Goths and other barbarians were still mucking around in Asia Minor. So in 276, Tacitus took an army there, drove out the barbarians, and then died (the cause is uncertain, but most authorities claim that he was murdered by officials who were worried about being punished for having killed one of Tacitus' relatives). The troops in Asia Minor promptly appointed Tacitus' associate (supposedly his half-brother) Florian to succeed him, but the army commander in Syria and Egypt, a general named Probus, nominated himself instead. After a few months during which Probus refused to engage Florian in a pitched battle, the latter's troops got sick of campaigning and killed him.

Probus spent the next six years dealing with revolts and invasions all over the empire, especially in Gaul. He did a pretty good job on the whole, but his luck ran out in 282, when he was knocked off and replaced by yet another general, Carus. Carus had two grown sons, Carinus and Numerian. Hoping to make his dynasty last more than a few years, he named Carinus co-emperor and left him in charge in the west while Carus himself, accompanied by Numerian, went east to attack Persia. Ever since Valerian's capture, the Romans had been itching to get revenge on the Persians, and since the

The City of Rome

You might be wondering, what with all the commotion on the frontiers in the late 3rd century, what was going on back in the city of Rome at the same time. After all, the city of Rome is where this history started, way back in Chapter One.

The answer is, the city was doing okay. Rich senators couldn't be generals anymore, but they could still get jobs in the civil administration if they wanted, or they could just enjoy life in their fancy townhouses and at their country estates. The emperors were too busy with wars to spend much time in Rome, but they kept supplying the poor people of Rome with free grain shipped in from Egypt and elsewhere. And Aurelian's wall turned out not to be necessary, for the moment, because no barbarians made it as far as Rome for over a century after the wall was built. The city may not have been the center of power anymore, but it was still a bustling metropolis, and still regarded by most citizens as the heart of the empire.

Persian king was now having troubles with rebels in his own country, this seemed like an opportune time to invade. Indeed, it was opportune: in 283, Carus led an army down the Tigris River and captured Ctesiphon, the capital of Persia's part of Iraq. But then Carus died, possibly from illness or assassination, or possibly, as several sources suggest, from being struck by a bolt of lightning. (Maybe Jupiter was mad because the Romans hadn't persecuted the Christians for a few decades). The troops lost heart upon the death of their commander and demanded that Numerian, now promoted to emperor, lead them back to the west. Numerian obliged, but then died himself on the way, in 284, quite possibly from natural causes. The army, however, thought he'd been murdered by his father-in-law, a general named Aper, and Aper was killed by yet another general named Diocles. The eastern army, impressed by Diocles' initiative, named him emperor on the spot; whereat, apparently thinking Diocles wasn't a long-enough name for an emperor, he changed his name to Diocletian. Of course, there was still another emperor, Carinus, back in the west, but after a battle between the two in the Balkans in 285, Carinus was dead and Diocletian reigned supreme.

Not that there was any reason to expect him to last very long, given how silly the succession had gotten in the last few decades. But it turned out that Diocletian had a few tricks up his sleeve. First, he recognized that Carus' idea of putting a junior partner in charge of one half of the empire had been a good one, since there were always invasions and rebellions going on all over the empire, and a lone emperor couldn't be everywhere at once. Having no sons, Diocletian first put a loyal general named Maximian in charge of the west, and then made it official by proclaiming him co-emperor in 286. Unfortunately, that same year, the commander of the fleet in the English Channel rebelled and took over both Britain and the northern coast of Gaul. Maximian, having no fleet left (and also confused by the term "English Channel," which hadn't even been invented yet), wasn't able to do much to suppress the rebellion. Besides, he was busy suppressing brigands and dealing with the Germans who kept crossing the Rhine to attack the empire. These Germans were now organized into several confederations, most notably the Alamanni in the south and the Franks and Saxons farther north. Maximian and his chief subordinate, a general named Constantius, managed to hold off the Germans but had to leave Britain alone for several years. Meanwhile, Diocletian was running all over the eastern half of the empire fighting foreign enemies and suppressing revolts, along the Danube, in Syria, and in Egypt. While in the Syria, he found time to persuade the Persians, chastened by Carus' earlier invasion, to let Armenia be a Roman client state again, instead of a Persian one, as it had been since Valerian's day.

Germans Crossing the Rhine

Apparently getting tired out by all this running around, Diocletian decided that two commanders-in-chief still wasn't enough, so in 293 he promoted Constantius to vice-emperor in the west while another guy named Galerius was made vice-emperor in the east. The vice-emperors had to divorce their wives and marry Maximian's and Diocletian's daughters, thus ensuring a dynastic succession when the emperors died or retired. Then Constantius, who took command of Gaul, got busy building a fleet and eventually was able to reconquer Britain, while Maximian went Africa to suppress rebels there, then settled down in northern Italy where he could keep an eye on the upper Danube. Galerius guarded the Balkans while Diocletian went to suppress another revolt in Egypt, but in 296 both Diocletian and Galerius had to go to Syria to ward off a Persian invasion led by a new and more pugnacious king. The Romans won the ensuing war convincingly, even sacking Ctesiphon again, and getting a peace treaty that recognized Rome's rule over Mesopotamia in northern Iraq as well as its protectorate over Armenia.

Clearly, this new plan of rule by four men (often called the Tetrarchy, from a Greek word meaning "rule by four men") was working out pretty well, mostly because the four men got along well together (as evidenced by a famous "group hug" statue of the four of them, in which they're even wearing cute matching outfits, complete with darling little hats). But it wasn't just the division of power that helped matters; Diocletian, who was still really the head honcho to whom the other tetrarchs deferred, also enacted some other reforms designed to ensure domestic tranquillity, provide for the common defense, promote the general welfare, etc., and incidentally to keep himself from getting assassinated. To begin with, he separated military and civilian administration in the provinces so that governors would be less able to rebel, and he subdivided the provinces so that military commanders, having smaller forces, would also have fewer resources for a rebellion. But at the same time, the overall size of the frontier army was increased somewhat, and lots of forts were built along the frontiers. Moreover, each of the tetrarchs had his own small reserve army, with a significant cavalry element, ready to rush to trouble spots as needed.

I Love You, You Love Me,
We're a Happy Tetrarchy

So much for military affairs, but emperors could be assassinated as well as overthrown. So Diocletian sought to promote a superstitious reverence for the imperial person by acting almost like a god on earth: rarely appearing in public, dressing in elaborate ceremonial clothing, and requiring those few people who were allowed to approach him to kiss his robe and address him as "Lord." He also tried to bring order to society by reforming and expanding the imperial bureaucracy, a move which probably did make government more effective, but also made it top-heavy and expensive. Luckily, relatively peaceful times meant that the economy had picked up a bit, so tax revenue was up enough to support the enlarged military and civil services. Diocletian even attempted to help the economy further by reforming the currency. Alas, his currency reform was only semi-successful, so next he tried to stem inflation by imposing wage-and-price controls. Naturally, that just led to a flourishing black market, and wage-and-price controls were soon abandoned. Despite these disappointments, the economy still did okay. Indeed, Diocletian and his successors collected enough tax revenue to be able to put up big new buildings in Rome, where construction of new public edifices had largely ground to a halt during the years of crisis. Diocletian even had enough money left over to build himself an enormous palace on the coast of the Adriatic Sea, a palace which would eventually serve as his retirement home.

Turning to social affairs, one of Diocletian's last acts, in 303, was to announce that it was time to start persecuting the Christians again. There hadn't been any official persecution for decades now, a lapse which made it possible for most people to realize that Christians, who were getting more numerous all the time, were mostly conscientious, loyal citizens, same as everyone else. Nevertheless, Galerius, a religious traditionalist, managed to persuade Diocletian that to cement the revival of Rome's fortunes, it was necessary for all citizens to take part in the old-time religion that had made Rome great in the first place. Since Christians refused to worship Jupiter or any other of the old gods, they had to be forced to see the error of their ways. Hence the persecution, which involved barring Christians from imperial employment, closing churches, burning Christian books, imprisoning church leaders, and sometimes killing Christians who refused to recant. However, the persecution was enforced with differing degrees of severity in different parts of the empire, depending on the prejudices of the tetrarchs and their various subordinates. In particular, Constantius, who had married a Christian woman before divorcing her to marry Maximian's daughter, went easy on her coreligionists.

Soon after the persecution got underway, Diocletian fell seriously ill and decided to resign, in 305. He ordered Maximian to resign at the same time, so that Galerius and Constantius could become co-emperors together. Appointed as new vice-emperors were two close associates of Galerius, Severus (about whom little is known) and Maximinus Daia (a.k.a. D-Max, an enthusiastic anti-Christian). Everyone went along with the change in regime, and the new system of government by Tetrarchy seemed like a brilliant success.

The Tetrarchy Is Not a Success

Uh-oh, turned out not everyone was happy with the new arrangements. Most notably, Constantius and Maximian both had sons, named Constantine and Maxentius respectively, who thought that they should have been named vice-emperors, not Severus and Daia. Thus, when Constantius died in 306 AD, his troops, loyal to his memory, proclaimed Constantine emperor. Not to be outdone, the Praetorian Guard, which still existed in reduced numbers as a sort of garrison for the city of Rome, seized the opportunity to once more take part in the emperor sweepstakes by enthroning Maxentius, who happened to be hanging around in Rome reminding everyone that he was the son of a well-respected ex-emperor. Galerius, outraged by this rampant unauthorized emperor-making, ordered Severus to attack Maxentius, Italy being a more proximate target than Gaul. However, Maxentius cleverly persuaded his father to come out of retirement, causing the troops to desert Severus in favor of their old commander, while Severus himself was captured and eventually executed. The next year, Maxentius forged an alliance with Constantine, quarreled with and deposed his own father, and beat off an attack on Italy led by Galerius himself.

Stymied, Galerius in 308 tried to win over Constantine by naming him official vice-emperor in the west. Galerius also appointed a supporter of his named Licinius as official emperor of the west, with control of the upper Danube region and orders to go kick Maxentius out of Italy. That didn't work either: Licinius decided not to attack Maxentius after all, plus Constantine and Maximinus Daia both decided they'd rather be emperors than vice-emperors, and accordingly so proclaimed themselves. That made five emperors at once, each ruling a different chunk of the empire, from west to east as follows: Constantine, Maxentius, Licinius, Galerius, Daia. And so matters rested for a few years.

Poor Galerius. Not only couldn't he impose his will on the other emperors, he couldn't even get most of those incomprehensible Christians to give up their religion, no matter how much he abused them. Finally, he gave up, in 311, publishing a decree granting Christians religious toleration and asking them to pray to their god for the welfare of the empire. Then, having presided over the complete collapse of the Tetrarchy, he died.

Naturally, Licinius and Daia immediately divided Galerius' territory between them. Since Daia got Asia Minor, the most valuable chunk, Licinius prudently decided to ally himself with Constantine. This alliance freed up Constantine to march into Italy in 312 and overthrow Maxentius. The decisive battle was fought near the Milvian Bridge outside of Rome, where Constantine's forces won a complete victory, and Maxentius was killed trying to flee the battlefield.

The battle of the Milvian Bridge is pretty famous, because Constantine supposedly had a vision the night before telling him to have his soldiers paint a Christian symbol on their shields if they wanted to win the battle. The son of Constantius' Christian first wife, Constantine was already sort of vaguely monotheistic, though he seems at this stage to have been unclear on whether he believed in the Christian god or the Unconquered Sun. But Christians took his victory as a sign of God's favor. Apparently, Constantine did likewise, since as soon as the Senate (impressed by the fact that he had a big army in the vicinity) proclaimed him senior emperor, he sent orders to Daia to stop the persecution of Christians that he'd been enforcing despite Galerius' edict of toleration. Daia grudgingly agreed, but then, when Licinius went to have a conference with his ally Constantine in Milan in 313, Daia led an army from Asia Minor into Europe to overthrow Licinius. Licinius hurried back to face him and won a battle in the Balkans. Daia retreated to Asia again, where, deserted by most of his followers, he died of disease (or maybe a broken heart) before Licinius could catch up with him.

In case you were wondering what ex-emperor Diocletian was doing during all the turmoil after his retirement, you'll be happy to know that he was enjoying his palatial seaside digs and resisting the temptation to come back and be emperor again. As we've seen, his co-ex-emperor, Maximian, was less prudent and ended up getting deposed by his own son. Maximian sought refuge with Constantine, but later he rebelled against Constantine and was executed in 310. Diocletian, on the other hand, lived several more years and died at home.

At this point, Constantine and Licinius must have read a copy of Chapter Five of this book, since, like Octavian and Antony, they decided against sharing the burden of government equally, and in favor of spending several years pushing and shoving to see who would become top dog. Or maybe Licinius didn't read Chapter Five, because if he had, he'd have known that the guy who ruled Italy and the western half of the empire was destined to win. The whole process was long and drawn out, so I'll spare you the details. Suffice it to say that Licinius was defeated and captured in 324, then executed in 325.

Voilà, the empire reunited under a single ruler; foreigners held at bay; economy and civil administration functioning reasonably well again; even epidemics less frequent than they had been. The Roman Empire was back! How did it happen? No doubt the tetrarchal system had provided a breathing space, and it also helped that the Germans were still usually more interested in pillage than in conquest. But the military reforms were probably the most important factor. The new army and its professional generals were once again a match for Persians, Germans, or anyone else in the vicinity, especially after Diocletian's reforms, so that eventually foreigners became less eager to try their hand at invading. Relative quiet on the frontiers helped promote a greater degree of stability and well-being throughout the empire. All in all, things may not have been as supercalifragilisticexpialidocious as they had been in the 2nd century, but, especially when we remember the troubles of the 3rd century, who could deny that things in early 4th century Rome looked at least califragilistic?

Examination Questions for Chapter Nine
answers will be gone through
when the test is returned

1. Define each of the following words. Use each one in a sentence.
   (a) *apotheosis*
   (b) *tetrarchy*
   (c) *expialidocious*

2. Consider the emperors Maximinus Thrax, Maximian, Maxentius, and Maximinus Daia. On the off chance that you remember any of their names a few years from now, do you think that you'll be able to remember which one was which? How about Constantius and Constantine? Galerius and Gallienus?

3. What day of the year do you suppose Aurelian established as the feast day of the Unconquered Sun?
   Hint: It's a few days after the winter solstice, when the sun, having seemed to get weaker and weaker as the days got shorter, now emerges triumphant and unconquered, as evidenced by the fact that the days are getting longer again.
   Another hint: The early Christian church, once it became ascendant in the Roman Empire, often put its holy days on the same days as pre-existing pagan holidays, so that people who were used to having a holiday on those days would be able to switch over to the Christian holiday without thinking about it too hard.
   Yet another hint: No one knows exactly what day of the year Jesus was born on. It doesn't say in the Bible (look for yourself if you don't believe me). Thus, early church leaders were free to put the celebration of Jesus' birth on any day of the year—say, for example, the date that was already being used by pagans to celebrate a different god of light.
   Last hint: The winter solstice normally falls on Dec. 21 or 22, which, interestingly, is just a few days before Christmas. (Christmas, in case you're not familiar with it, is a Christian holiday commemorating the birth of Jesus. It's celebrated on Dec. 25 every year.)

   DISCLAIMER
   (SPECIALLY INCLUDED TO PRE-EMPT COMPLAINTS FROM ANY AUSSIES WHO ARE STILL UPSET ABOUT BEING CALLED SUBJECTS OF QUEEN ELIZABETH BACK IN THE PREVIOUS CHAPTER) YES, I'M AWARE THAT IN THE SOUTHERN HEMISPHERE, THE WINTER SOLSTICE IS IN JUNE, NOT DECEMBER. YIPPEE. HOWEVER, THE ROMANS DIDN'T LIVE THE SOUTHERN HEMISPHERE.

4. Guess what Constantine's mother's name was.
   Hint: The island where the British deposited Napoleon in 1815 was named after Constantine's mother. See, Napoleon's appearance on the map at the beginning of the chapter wasn't completely inappropriate, just mostly so.

Citizens of the Roman Empire!

Are you looking for a ***new home*** at a ***great price***?

Then look no further! Emperor Constantine has a deal for you!

That's right, having liberated the east from the tyrant Licinius, our illustrious ruler is building a ***brand new city*** on the site of the ancient Greek city of Byzantium.

And it shall be called…

CONSTANTINOPLE

Or, if you prefer, you can call it ***New Rome***. The emperor likes that name too.

And it will indeed be a new Rome, an eastern capital for our mighty empire.

Emperor Constantine himself will live there in a ***palace***
suitable for so magnificent a potentate.

Like old Rome, the new city will have its own ***Senate***, luxurious ***public baths***,
a ***chariot-racing stadium***, numerous ***Christian churches***,
and of course, ***free food*** for poor citizens.

PEACE OF MIND
Constantinople will be a gated community, with a city wall and its own security force.

LOCATION, LOCATION, LOCATION
On the European coast just across from Asia Minor, between the Black Sea and the Aegean Sea, Constantinople is perfectly located not just for an emperor who wants to keep watch on the eastern and western half of his dominions, but also for a regular citizen like you!

So what are you waiting for? Pack your bags and get moving today!

LEGAL NOTICE: THE BUILDERS OF CONSTANTINOPLE ASSUME NO LIABILITY FOR DAMAGES DUE TO EARTHQUAKES. IT'S NOT OUR FAULT THE EMPEROR WANTS TO BUILD HIS NEW CAPITAL IN AN EARTHQUAKE ZONE. WE RECOMMEND TRYING TO GET EARTHQUAKE INSURANCE.

THE HISTORY OF ROME

Chapter Ten

in which our story comes to an end, sometime or other

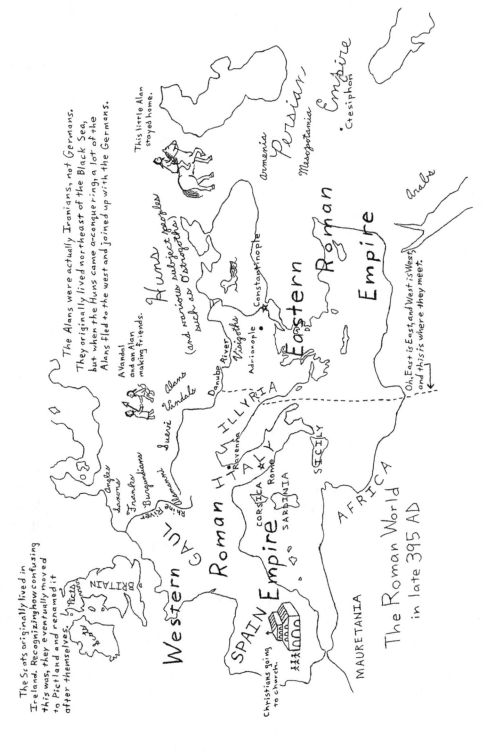

The Scots originally lived in Ireland. Recognizing how confusing this was, they eventually moved to Pictland and renamed it after themselves.

Christians going to church.

The Alans were actually Iranians, not Germans. They originally lived northeast of the Black Sea, but when the Huns came a-conquering, a lot of the Alans fled to the west and joined up with the Germans.

A Vandal and an Alan making friends.

This little Alan stayed home.

Oh, East is East, and West is West, and this is where they meet.

The Roman World in late 395 AD

Picts

BRITAIN

Angles
Saxons
Franks
Burgundians
Alemanni
Rhine River
Suevi
Vandals
Alans

Huns
(and various subject peoples such as Ostrogoths)

Danube River

Western

Roman

GAUL

ILLYRIA

ITALY

Ravenna

Rome

CORSICA

SARDINIA

Visigoths

SICILY

Adrianople

Constantinople

Eastern

Roman

Empire

Empire

SPAIN

Empire

AFRICA

MAURETANIA

Armenia

Persian

Mesopotamia

Empire

Ctesiphon

Arabs

Why This is the Last Chapter in the Book

There's a tendency among historians to give short shrift to the late Roman Empire; i.e., the time from the reign of Constantine till the empire's fall. Indeed, some historians are so lazy that, in order to avoid having to write Chapter Ten of their histories at all, they declare that when Constantine moved the capital to Constantinople in the Greek-speaking east, the empire ceased to be Roman, leaving the historians free to go home early and down some whisky.

Sounds like a cop-out to me. Yes, Constantine dissolved the Praetorian Guard, diverted some of the grain supply of Rome to Constantinople, and gave Constantinople its own Senate to complement the Roman one. But Rome remained the biggest and most prestigious city in the empire, and even if most emperors didn't live there anymore (they normally hung out near the frontiers, or else in Constantinople), they still visited occasionally. They also kept paying for public entertainments, construction of new buildings, sewer and road repair, and so on. Constantine himself put up a great big triumphal arch near the Colosseum—you can still see it today if you go to visit Rome. In fact, the traditional date for the fall of Rome, well-known even to lazy historians, is 476 AD, over a hundred years after Constantine's death. Admittedly, 476 AD is just as controversial a date as 753 BC for the founding of Rome, 509 BC for the establishment of the Republic, or 27 BC for the creation of the empire. But 476 is still the date that everybody knows, and since this book has to end sometime, that's when it's going to be (hope I didn't ruin the suspense). Besides, as we'll see later in the chapter, there are good arguments in favor of the traditional date, and there's certainly no agreement on any alternative.

The Arch of Constantine

On the other hand, as long as I'm following tradition here, I'm going to give, at best, only medium shrift to the late empire. My reasons for this are pretty much the same as everyone else's: the late empire isn't as much fun as what came before. Oh, sure, there's the occasional crank like Edward Gibbon, who wrote a giant multi-volume work that didn't end till the Turks captured Constantinople in 1453. However, few people read Gibbon's whole book nowadays, though some pretend to have done so in order to impress other people at cocktail parties. The limited readership is understandable: people who are interested in the Romans probably want to read about their glory days, as opposed to slogging through an enormous tome whose theme is a millennium of decline.

But even if we limit ourselves to pre-476 Rome, the late empire was less fun than what preceded it, for reasons hinted at in the previous chapter. Carrying on in the Diocletianic tradition, Constantine and his successors were unabashed autocrats, and the government was a centralized despotism in which all power flowed from the top. However, since the emperors were isolated by their lofty position, cut off from their own people by elaborate ceremony and hordes of courtiers, the expanded imperial bureaucracy actually ran things on a day-to-day basis. There were no elections, and little accountability to the people being governed. Even town councillors were appointed by higher-ranking officials, who naturally allowed bribes and/or personal connections to influence their choices; after all, bribes and personal influence were what had gotten the higher-ranking officials into office themselves. Thus nepotism and corruption flourished, and the emperors, who got most of their information from courtiers and bureaucrats, could do little to restrain governmental malfeasance.

The imperial court, the expanded and corrupt bureaucracy, and in particular the army, which, as we've seen, was bigger and thus more expensive than ever, all needed money. That meant continued high taxation by a government that had become fairly efficient at squeezing its subjects. Poor and middle class people were squeezed the hardest, because the rich could bribe the tax collectors or put together armed gangs to intimidate them, especially out in the countryside where government influence was weak. Wealthy landholders got even more wealthy whenever poor peasants, who needed protection not just from tax collectors, but also from rampaging barbarians and home-grown bandits, sold their land to rich aristocrats and became tenant farmers with limited civil rights. The government did little to help the poor peasants, which makes sense given that most higher-ranking civilian officials were themselves wealthy landholders who benefited from the peasants' misfortune.

It's true that things hadn't always been great for the poor back in the old days, either; frankly, things are often not so great for the poor, all over the world. But at least under the Republic and early empire, we could be distracted by the spectacle of Rome's rise to power, its conquest of lots of enemy nations, and the establishment of peace and unity in the Mediterranean world. The late empire, by contrast, didn't conquer anybody, nor was there much peace or unity, what with frequent civil wars and attacks by foreigners. It is true, though, that the army was able to hold off the foreigners pretty well for most of the 4th century. Constantine shrank the size and status of the legions on the frontiers while increasing the size of the mobile reserves, which were stationed at a few strategic places around the empire. This seemed to work well, but it was hard to find enough men to keep the army up to strength, since the population had declined in the 3rd century, and since being a soldier was a rough and dangerous trade in this warmongering era. In addition, peasant farmers were needed to grow crops, and townsfolk had their own economically important work to do. So, to keep both the army and the civilian economy functioning, emperors from Diocletian onward decreed that sons should follow their fathers' trades: soldiers' sons had to be soldiers, tenant farmers' sons were stuck farming the same land as their fathers, and so on. To be sure, not everyone was bound to his father's profession in this way, and even those who were officially bound often flouted the law in the same way as they undoubtedly cheated on their taxes. Still, this sort of regimented society isn't very attractive to most people nowadays, apart from die-hard communists.

Moreover, like communism, the regimentation system didn't really work as planned, so that emperors had to make up for shortages of soldiers or peasants by hiring barbarian warriors or resettling defeated tribesmen in underpopulated agricultural districts. In economic terms, such policies had much to recommend them, provided the barbarians remained obedient to Roman authority. Moreover, since the barbarians, especially Germans, were redoubtable warriors who would fight against you if they had nothing else to do with their time, it made sense in military terms to pay them to fight for you instead.

Nevertheless, you couldn't expect most Germans to feel the sort of patriotic fervor that the citizen body had displayed back in the old days. Then again, in the 4th and 5th centuries, most citizens weren't too hopping-up-and-down fervent themselves. After all, this was a country that asked not what it could do for its citizens, but what its citizens could do for it—then answered, "What you can do is shut up, pay your taxes, and revere the emperor."

But let's not get to thinking that everyone was unhappy with 4th-5th century life. Rich landowners, as we've seen, did quite well, especially senators in the west, some of whom had incomes of thousands of pounds of gold each year. And gold it was, too, because Constantine enacted a successful currency reform based on gold coinage, thus prompting a revival of trade that benefited cities across the empire. So even middle-class people were doing okay in a lot of those cities. Moreover, middle-class people with a bit of education could join the civil service, a source of income, security, and eventually status if you could get yourself promoted to a high-ranking job. Indeed, successful civil servants could even become senators, once emperors after Constantine decided that senator should be a title, rather than a job, and started naming influential people senators in droves regardless of whether they ever stopped by the senate house to deliver an oration. There wasn't much point to delivering orations anyway, since emperors were more likely to listen to advice from wives and flunkeys than from senatorial speechifiers.

One of Constantine's
Gold Coins

So life wasn't all bad in the late empire, even when the empire started breaking apart in the 5th century. Who knows, maybe everyday life was actually better for most people than it had been in Caesar's day, when politics was murderous, civil wars were bloody, and non-citizens were ruthlessly oppressed. But you don't have to watch the *Star Wars* movies to know that most modern-day people have an instinctive preference for a republic over a despotic empire. Heck, even the art and literature of the late Roman Empire are less pleasing to modern tastes than the earlier stuff. Portraiture, for example, became less naturalistic and more symbolic as time went on, as seen in the rather stiff and unlifelike statue of the tetrarchs in the last chapter, or in various images of Constantine that show him gazing heavenward with big weird eyes. As for literature, although it continued to be written, even during the troubled 3rd century, little of it is read today. A lot of it is considered pretty bad quality, and even the better-written stuff, like the work of the outstanding 4th century historian Ammianus Marcellinus, is nowhere near as popular as Tacitus or Vergil.

There is, however, one important exception in the area of literature, namely, Christian literature. Which brings us to one last major difference between the late empire and earlier Roman society: the late empire was Christian. That doesn't mean that everyone in the empire was a Christian. Indeed, when Constantine came to power, the Christians were still just a relatively small minority, though an influential one, since they were concentrated in the cities and so had a fairly high profile. But their numbers grew when Constantine became sole emperor and started promoting the worship of the god who, in his opinion, had brought him to power. With only one short-lived exception, all the emperors after Constantine were Christians too, and they all did things like building churches, exempting clergymen from taxation, promoting Christians to high office, and so on. Eventually, they went farther, looting and destroying temples, banning public celebration of pagan rituals, and barring non-Christians from government service. It's no surprise, then, that Christianity flourished in the late empire. But apart from material considerations, Christianity also had an intellectual energy that fuelled its growth, an energy which manifested itself in writings that are still widely read today. I won't go through all of the authors in question—this is a history of Rome, not a history of Christianity—but I will mention two of the most famous, both of whom wrote in Latin. The first is St. Jerome, a cantankerous 4th-5th century scholar whose Latin version of the Bible, known as the Vulgate, was the standard scriptural text of the Roman Catholic Church until the 1960's. The second is St. Augustine, a near contemporary of Jerome whose theological masterwork, *The City of God*, is too long to be superpopular now that we have television to distract us. On the other hand,

Augustine's autobiography, *The Confessions*, is still read today by millions of undergraduate students who don't understand why the middle-aged Augustine was so hung up on that time he stole some pears as a teenager.

So, to sum up: lack of glorious conquests; overbearing rich people; really overbearing emperors; corrupt bureaucratic state; patriotism on the wane; decline of secular culture; and frontiers still harassed by aggressive foreigners. Throw in the fact that, with the benefit of hindsight, we know that disaster is going to overtake the empire in the 5th century, and you can see why the late empire has usually been considered less fun to write about than what preceded it. Heck, even bad emperors from the old days, like Caligula or Elagabalus, were at least colorful, as opposed to a milquetoast like Honorius (whom we'll meet later in this chapter). I should, however, point out that a number of recent historians have tried to reverse the judgment of their predecessors by saying that the late empire is fascinating, worth at least three or four chapters in a book like this one, and maybe worth ten or twenty chapters. I'm not buying it. One chapter, yes: again I denounce those lazy bums who think that they can stop with the reign of Constantine, and who are probably drunk by now while I'm still writing this chapter and you're still reading it. But one chapter is good enough, just like one chapter was plenty for getting us from Rome's founding to 201 BC. So, having finally gotten through the introduction to this chapter, let's get back to our narrative and find out who conquered whom, who got assassinated, which emperors were wimps, and finally, when, how, and why the Roman Empire fell. (Actually, we already know when. 476 AD. But we still need to find out how and why.)

From Constantine to Theodosius

Constantine liked Constantinople so much that once he moved in, he pretty much stayed there, leaving his subordinates to watch the frontiers. That gave the emperor time to try to settle abstruse theological debates between different factions of Christians—with little success, seeing as Constantine himself could rarely determine for certain which side he thought was right Then he got distracted by other business in the 330's when the Persians decided it was about time to attack Armenia again, and Mesopotamia for good measure. Constantine began preparing for war but then died in 337.

With Constantine dead, the empire was quickly divided among his three sons: Constantine II, who got Britain, Gaul, and Spain; Constans, who got Italy, Africa, and Illyria; and Constantius II, who got everything east of Constans. Constantine II, the oldest son, was apparently upset with the size of his portion, because in 340 he invaded Italy in an attempt to depose Constans. Instead, Constantine was killed in battle, and Constans got to add the far west to his territory. Constantius, meanwhile, was too busy holding off Persian attacks on Mesopotamia to care about which brother ruled the west. However,

A Deathbed Conversion?

Constantine I wasn't baptized until he was on his deathbed, leading some confused modern commentators to suspect that he was never very sincere in his Christianity. Actually, in those days, it was common to hold off on baptism as long as possible. Early Christians, like modern ones, believed in one baptism for the forgiveness of sins. But unlike later Christians, early Christians hadn't developed the idea that you can get absolved of your sins by means of confession and penance. That meant that only baptism, which was a one-time deal, could get you off the hook. So, rather than be baptized early in life and then get stuck with any sins they committed thereafter, many people waited to get baptized until they had little chance left to commit any new, unerasable sins. As for Constantine, he'd given up on the Unconquered Sun and was clearly a sincere Christian long before his death.

113

Constantius did care when Constans was deposed and killed in 350 in a coup led by a general named Magnentius. Luckily, after over a decade of failure to conquer anything, the Persians had decided to take a break, leaving Constantius free to march west and confront Magnentius. The ensuing civil war was uncharacteristically long and bloody, but by 353 Magnentius was dead and Constantius was sole emperor. Trying to ensure future loyalty in the west, Constantius named his cousin Julian vice-emperor and put him in charge of Gaul, where the Franks and Alamanni were causing trouble again. Julian, despite being a twenty-something intellectual with no prior military experience, thrashed the Germans pretty severely. Meanwhile, Constantius himself went to visit Rome, a city he'd never seen before, then headed back east in time to be in Constantinople in 359 when news came that the Persians were done with their timeout and ready to rumble.

Faced with this new threat, Constantius quite properly ordered Julian to send some of his troops east to help out. The troops, who didn't want to go east, suggested that Julian declare himself emperor instead, which Julian thought was an excellent idea. Constantius, however, objected to having a self-appointed co-emperor; therefore, after consolidating his rule in the west, Julian marched east in 361 to depose his cousin. In the event, Constantius died of natural causes while Julian was still en route. Without even fighting a battle, the twenty-something intellectual had gotten to be emperor of the whole schmeer.

And quite a shocking emperor he turned out to be, from the standpoint of the very Christian city of Constantinople, where he arrived late in the year. It turned out that Julian, who had been raised a Christian, had secretly converted to paganism during his student days—specifically, to Neoplatonism, a fairly recent amalgamation of Greek philosophy, traditional polytheism, and magical practices. Now that he was emperor, Julian openly promoted the worship of the old gods and tried to suppress Christianity, though he wasn't in a strong enough position to launch a full-blown persecution. To little avail—it turned out that few Greek-speaking easterners shared Julian's love of ancient Greek philosophers, and that in fact, Christianity was doing well not just because of government support, but because people actually believed in it.

Well, maybe Julian could be more successful in foreign affairs than domestically. He thought so, anyway. Two of his heroes were Alexander the Great and Trajan, and since the Persians were already at war with Rome, Julian decided to put together a great big army and launch a major invasion. It took a while to get everything ready, but in 363 he and the troops set forth, trumpets a-sounding. They reached the Persian capital of Ctesiphon in central Iraq, but found it too well garrisoned to be taken by storm, while the Romans were short of supplies and under constant harassment by guerrilla forces. The army was forced to try to withdraw through hostile territory, skirmishing as it went, and in one of the skirmishes, Julian was killed.

The emperorless troops quickly chose a successor, an officer named Jovian, whose first achievement was to strike a deal with the Persians: in return for letting the Roman army go home alive, Persia got to take over most of Mesopotamia and Armenia. Jovian's second achievement was to announce, once he got back to Roman territory, that paganism was out and Christianity was in again, this time for good, since all the emperors from Jovian onward were Christians. His third achievement was to die in late 363, leaving the way open for a more distinguished successor.

The successor chosen by military and civilian bigwigs was a general named Valentinian, who promptly named his brother Valens co-emperor. Valens stayed in the east, while Valentinian went west and spent a decade dealing successfully with barbarian incursions, not just along the Rhine and upper Danube, but also in Britain and Africa. Then he died of a stroke in

375, and was succeeded by his young adult son Gratian (also supposedly by Gratian's little brother Valentinian II, but since Valentinian II was only four years old, he wasn't a very hands-on administrator). Valens, in the meantime, had been busy putting down a serious revolt early in his reign, making a deal with the Goths to keep peace on the lower Danube, and resuscitating the squabble with the Persians over Armenia. (It must have been confusing to be an Armenian in ancient times. Did they have to write little notes to themselves and carry them around in case they forgot whether they were pro-Roman or pro-Persian on any particular day of the week? That's what I would have done.)

Overall, despite Julian's stupid invasion of Persia, things seemed to be going pretty well for the empire. As per the usual pattern in this history, that was a sign that things were about to get very bad. The root cause of the oncoming badness was the Huns, barbarians from somewhere in east-central Asia who liked to gallop around on horses herding sheep and shooting arrows at people. They were master horsemen and master archers, and when some of them came galloping into the region north of the Black Sea, the Goths who'd set up kingdoms there didn't have a chance. Down went the Gothic kingdoms like houses of cards, or ships of fools, or something, and the Goths themselves ended up either as subjects of the Huns or as refugees heading west to join their Gothic brethren north of the Danube. Soon afterward, in 376 AD, came terrifying reports

Here Come the Huns

that the Huns were coming after them. The refugees and their brethren came up with the bright idea of crossing the Danube and hiding behind the Roman frontier; after all, they were at peace with the Romans now, weren't they? To get permission to immigrate, they told Valens that if he let them cross and gave them land, they'd be both loyal soldiers and productive farmers.

Valens recognized that the Goths would make a useful addition to the imperial army, but he was worried about letting so many barbarians past the frontiers. Finally he decided to let some but not all of them across. However, such migrations are hard to control, and a lot more came over than were supposed to, causing Valens, now even more worried, to dilly-dally about finding land for them. The Goths, who were short on food and suspicious of Valens' promises, started pillaging local villages. Naturally, the local army commander tried to stop them, but the Goths were in a fighting mood and crushed the Roman troops. Then they started pillaging all over the Balkans, just like in the bad old days of the 3rd century.

With a heavy sigh, Valens got to work trying to defeat the pesky plunderers. After desultory fighting in 377, he collected a large army in 378 and faced the main Gothic army near the city of Adrianople. It was Cannae all over again: the overconfident Romans were crushed, losing two-thirds of their men, including the emperor himself. Bummer.

The only silver lining was that the Goths, like Hannibal, weren't much good at besieging fortified cities, though that did little to comfort the villagers who were now subject to merciless pillaging. Gratian, who was still pretty young and inexperienced, and anyway busy with the usual barbarian raids in the west, decided to appoint an experienced general named Theodosius as co-emperor with orders to go fix things in the Balkans. Theodosius was hampered by lack of troops—remember, most of the eastern field army had been slaughtered at Adrianople, and it was hard to recruit replacements when potential recruits knew that joining the army meant fighting the ferocious Goths. The new emperor eventually had to let a lot more barbarians join the army than in times past, and even then he was unable to crush the invaders. On the other hand, the Goths, unable to capture major cities and not sure what to do next, remembered that all they'd wanted in the first place was the right to settle somewhere south of the Danube. Thus, in 382, the two sides reached an agreement: the Goths got land to live on within the frontiers, under their own laws and own chieftains, without paying taxes to Rome, but with the responsibility of fighting on Theodosius' behalf when called upon. Maybe that was the best Theodosius could do under the circumstances; at least the Goths settled down for a little while. Neverthless, there was now an effectively independent barbarian nation inside the empire, which you know can't be a good thing.

Back in the west, Gratian, a fervent Christian, was annoying the Senate by his anti-pagan measures; western senators, whose position in society depended on respect for Rome's traditions, naturally tended to be traditionalists in religion. Soldiers, on the other hand, were less annoyed by Gratian's religious policy than by his unmilitary character. Unsurprisingly, it was a soldier, the Roman commander in Britain (named, somewhat ridiculously, Magnus Maximus, which is Latin for "Great Greatest"), who eventually rebelled, in 383. He then invaded Gaul, where Gratian was defeated and killed. A few years later Maximus and his troops tromped into Italy, causing young Valentinian II to flee to Theodosius' domain. In reply, Theodosius marched west in 388, defeated and killed Maximus, and reinstalled Valentinian. But then in 392, Valentinian quarrelled with his chief general, a Frank named Arbogast who had risen high in Roman service. Valentinian died right after the quarrel, supposedly by suicide, but I don't suppose Arbogast commissioned an independent inquiry to confirm the verdict. Since Arbogast, being of barbarian origin, couldn't be emperor himself, he appointed a conservative senator named Eugenius as his puppet and demanded that Theodosius recognize Eugenius as co-emperor. Instead, Theodosius marched back to Italy in 394, defeated and killed his enemies, then got sick and died in early 395.

Barbarians Galore

Theodosius was the last emperor to rule over a united Roman Empire. When he died, his teenage son Arcadius became emperor in the east, while Arcadius' ten-year-old brother Honorius became emperor in the west. Even after they grew up, both boys were wimpy emperors who sat around in their palaces while generals and courtiers fought for power amongst themselves. It was during this period that the eastern and western halves of the empire definitely started to go their own separate ways. The eastern half was more fortunate in that, although the Balkans were still troubled, the Persians had their own problems with barbarians coming out of central Asia, and so the Roman-Persian frontier was mostly peaceful during the 5th century. Our focus from here on out, therefore, will be mostly on the western empire, since that's where the action was, and also since the western empire was the more Roman half, as opposed to the Greek east.

The effective ruler in the west after Theodosius' death was a general named Stilicho, a German whose position was a reward for his loyal service under Theodosius. Similarly loyal service had been provided by the Goths of the Balkans (who hereafter can be called Visigoths to distinguish them from their north-of-the-Danube brethren, whom we'll call Ostrogoths). Indeed, when Theodosius invaded Italy in 388 and 394, the Visigoths had even kept their promise to send troops to help him. But now old Theo was dead, and the Visigoths felt unappreciated. So, led by a fellow named Alaric, who was envious of Stilicho's success in getting a high-ranking job in the Roman army, they started rampaging through the Balkans again. Stilicho brought an army over to stop them, but he got little cooperation from the eastern empire, whose leaders were worried that an overly-successful Stilicho would try to gain hegemony over east as well as west. After a couple of years of inconclusive fighting, Stilicho gave up and went back to Italy. The eastern empire then pacified Alaric by appointing him to a generalship in Illyria, which meant that he got a nice salary and his troops got supplies courtesy of the Roman government.

Unfortunately, Alaric doesn't seem to have liked Illyria very much, because just a few years later, in 401, he decided to march into Italy and try his luck there. However, Stilicho strengthened his army by the addition of troops pulled out of Britain and Gaul, and after a bloody but inconclusive battle in 402, the Visigoths had to return to Illyria in a grumpy mood.

Meanwhile, north of the Danube, momentous events were occurring. After their defeat of the Goths in the 370's, the Huns had settled down for a while. But eventually some of them got restless and started moving up the Danube, killing and conquering the people in their path. Those locals who weren't killed or conquered fled to the west, where they eventually bumped into the Roman frontier. There they found that, what with Stilicho's withdrawal of troops to help in the defense of Italy, the frontier wasn't well-defended. Unsurprisingly, the barbarian refugees decided to jump right over the ill-defended border in order to get to the Hun-free zone on the other side.

Huns II: Sons of the Huns

The first ones across, in 405, were some Ostrogoths who made the mistake of going into northern Italy, which is where Stilicho was hanging around with his army. So the Ostrogoths were quickly defeated, but the next year some cleverer tribes, known as Suevi, Alans, and Vandals, crossed the Rhine into Gaul instead. At the same time, Britain, short on troops just like Gaul, was being harassed by barbarians from Ireland and northern Britain known as Scots and Picts, respectively, not to mention Saxons who rowed over from the northern coast of Germany. The Romano-Britons decided to proclaim their own emperor in hopes that he could rectify the situation, but all he did was gather up all the remaining Roman troops and cross over to Gaul in 407, by which time Gaul was flat-out infested with barbarians.

Emperor Honorius by now was hiding out in Ravenna, a city in northern Italy that was almost impregnable to assault because it was surrounded by swamps. Stilicho, not wanting to leave Italy lest Alaric's grumpy Visigoths return, was unable to reconquer Gaul, and soon began losing support among Roman aristocrats. In 408, these aristocrats persuaded Honorius to execute Stilicho, along with a lot of his barbarian soldiers, who were presumed to be more loyal to their commander than to the empire.

The massacre backfired in a big way, since most of the surviving barbarians quickly deserted the Roman army and joined up with Alaric, who, the moment he heard that Stilicho was dead, had marched into Italy. The remnants of the Roman army were too weak to stop him, but since Ravenna was impregnable, the Visigoths marched on Rome instead. Alaric didn't really want to capture Rome; his actual purpose was, by threatening the city, to put pressure on

Honorius to give land and cash to him and his followers. Unfortunately, it turned out that Honorius, safe in Ravenna, didn't care if Rome got captured or not; either way, he stubbornly refused to negotiate with the Visigothic leader. Befuddled, Alaric and his army spent the next two years wandering around Italy, accomplishing little beyond extorting money from the locals. Finally, in 410, he said the hell with it, he was going to capture Rome and see what happened.

What happened was that the whole Roman world was shocked. Rome, capital city of the mighty Roman Empire, captured by barbarians for the first time since the Gauls did it in 390 BC! Oh, what a calamity! That's what most people thought, anyway, but Honorius apparently thought, "Big deal. I'm still not giving him any land." All the Visigoths got out of Rome was whatever they could carry off in three days of looting. Next, Alaric decided they should go south and try to get to Africa, which had lots of fertile land. But his ships got sunk in a storm before the Visigoths could get on board, and then Alaric died. His successor, recognizing that this bouncing-around-Italy thing was getting the Visigoths nowhere, decided to take them north to Gaul.

Italy breathed a sigh of relief, but there was plenty of action farther west over the next several years: there were several rebellions by local Roman leaders; the Suevi, Alans, and Vandals stormed into Spain; Britain, abandoned by the Roman army, became effectively independent; the Visigoths wandered around and managed to fight with almost every other faction in Gaul or Spain at one time or another; and even the court at Ravenna was able to raise new armies and get into the game again. Indeed, somewhat surprisingly, Honorius' officials managed to play the different factions off against each other so effectively that, by the time the dust settled in 418, the Alans were mostly wiped out, the Suevi and Vandals were bottled up in northwestern Spain, the Visigoths were settled as Roman allies in southwestern Gaul, and the rest of Gaul was officially under central government authority again. The key to this success was that the imperial government had finally promised land to the Visigoths, provided the Visigoths would help the empire deal with its other enemies. The Visigoths agreed, the alliance worked, and the western empire was still alive.

On the other hand, Britain was no longer part of the empire. In addition, our old friends the Franks and Alamanni, along with another Germanic tribe called the Burgundians, had taken advantage of the turmoil to grab large chunks of eastern Gaul. Northwestern Gaul was in a state of civil disorder, and wasn't likely to yield any taxes to a cash-strapped central authority. The Suevi and Vandals were by no means inclined to keep the peace, and we've already seen how reliable the Visigoths were as allies in the long term. Plus the whole of western Europe had been devastated by the fighting; Rome had been sacked by barbarians; and the pathetic Honorius was still emperor. The western empire was still alive, but it wasn't exactly doing handsprings.

Aetius and Attila

While the west was being ravaged by barbarians, the east, once the Visigoths left the Balkans, was enjoying relative peace and attendant prosperity. Arcadius died in 408 AD and was succeeded by his son Theodosius II. Back in the west, Honorius died in 423, leaving no sons, and a high-ranking bureaucrat at Rome claimed the western crown. But Honorius and Arcadius had had a sister, Galla Placidia, who had a son named Valentinian. Loyal to his family, in 425 Theodosius dispatched an army to Italy which deposed the bureaucrat and installed six-year-old Valentinian as Emperor Valentinian III.

Naturally, a six-year-old emperor doesn't spend a lot of time on affairs of state, so various generals and bureaucrats spent the next eight years fighting each other for power. The eventual winner was a general named Aetius, who, upon becoming de facto ruler of the west, faced a difficult situation. While the Romans were fighting each other, the Germans in Gaul had taken the opportunity to expand their territories. In addition, the Vandals, under the leadership of a king named Gaiseric, had left Spain and conquered Mauretania in 429, while the Suevi took to raiding the Roman-held parts of Spain.

Aetius, deciding that Gaul was the first priority, spent the 430's fighting the Visigoths, Franks, Alamanni, and Burgundians. He was largely successful in getting them to stop being so belligerent, but then in 439 disaster struck when the Vandals moved east from Mauretania and conquered Roman Africa (which, you'll remember, means basically modern Tunisia). This prosperous region was an important source of food for Italy and of tax revenue for the central government; it was also the home base of the western empire's fleet. The eastern empire, just as worried about this development as Aetius was, sent a fleet and some troops to help Aetius drive the Vandals out of Africa again. But the joint expedition which set out in 441 had to turn back after getting only as far as Sicily, because suddenly the eastern empire had more pressing problems.

The Huns, who originally were a bunch of loosely allied tribal groups, had gotten themselves organized into a single kingdom in the early 5th century. Now they had a new king named Attila (finally, a 5th-century guy that you've actually heard of before). In 441, taking advantage of the absence of a lot of eastern troops on the African expedition, Attila and his Huns stormed across the Danube and plundered like nobody's business. They fought with the eastern empire for most of the decade, till Theodosius bought them off with the immediate

> The Huns are not the ancestors of the Hungarians, whose name for themselves is "Magyars." The word "Hungarian" derives from the name "On Ogur," meaning 'Ten Arrows,' the name of a Magyar confederacy in the early Middle Ages.

payment of 6000 pounds of gold and the promise of 2100 pounds per year thereafter. Happy with that arrangement, Attila promptly headed west to see what the pickings were like in Gaul. To Attila's chagrin, Aetius organized a coalition of Romans, Visigoths, Franks, and Burgundians that drove back the Hunnish invasion in 451. Next year, Attila invaded Italy instead, where there weren't any Visigoths, Franks, or

Huns III: The Scourge of God

Burgundians to help out the Romans, and captured several cities. But disease and famine were weakening his army, and the eastern empire (under a new and more vigorous emperor, who'd replaced Theodosius when the latter died in 450) was threatening the Hunnish lands in the east. So the Huns pulled back to central Europe, where Attila died in 453. Without its dynamic leader, the Hunnish dominion collapsed as the Ostrogoths and other subject peoples rose up against their masters and sent them fleeing back east like scared rabbits, or at least like scared Huns.

The Fall of the Roman Empire

Loss of Africa notwithstanding, Aetius was clearly riding high after Attila's death. But Italian aristocrats were upset with him for not defending Italy as successfully as Gaul, and Valentinian III was worried that his successful general might be planning to depose him. Thus, in 454, egged on by a senator named Petronius Maximus, Valentinian personally stabbed Aetius to death. The next year, two of Aetius' former bodyguards avenged Aetius by assassinating Valentinian. And chaos descended on the Roman Empire.

The main activity of the next twenty years was a constant struggle among various factions to try to choose the next emperor, or to depose an emperor that some other faction had put into power. The reason for all this activity was that the imperial office still had prestige, access to some tax revenue, and the instinctive support of many citizens—hence the struggle over whose candidate would get the job. The leading factions were: the eastern empire; the three main Roman armies in the west, headquartered in Gaul, Italy, and Illyria, respectively; the wealthy aristocrats of the city of Rome; and the Germanic kingdoms of southern Gaul and Africa, i.e., the Visigoths, Burgundians, and Vandals. The most successful participant in the game was Ricimer, a German who commanded the Roman army in Italy, and who made and unmade emperors almost at will. He was less successful, though, at defending Italy from the Vandals, who used their fleet to harass the coasts and even sacked Rome in 455, while the empire was still in a muddle because of the recent deaths of Aetius and Valentinian. The Vandals even conquered Sardinia, Corsica, and part of Sicily, while Gaul and Spain slipped out of imperial control and into the hands of local German or Roman rulers. After Ricimer's death in 472, a few more emperors were installed and disinstalled by different factions, the last one being a general's son named Romulus (nicknamed Augustulus, meaning "little Augustus," because he was only a child). Alas, the Italian army, whose soldiers were now mostly Germans, rebelled in 476 because the government couldn't afford to pay them. Led by an German officer named Odoacer, the troops deposed Romulus (but he wasn't killed, because the soldiers took pity on his youth), and Odoacer announced that he was now King of Italy, and there wouldn't be any more of this silly emperor stuff in the west. Officially, Odoacer recognized the authority of the eastern empire, which was still going strong, but in reality Italy was independent, as was the rest of the west.

> When the Vandals sacked Rome, they looted the city, including its many Catholic churches, very thoroughly before going back to Africa. In the 18th century, during the French Revolution, a bishop who knew Roman history coined the term "vandalism" to refer to the looting and wanton destruction that atheistic revolutionaries were visiting upon French churches.

And that was the end of the Roman Empire. Of course, some historians argue that it didn't really fall in 476, but I say that it did, and if they don't like it, they'll have to write their own books (actually, some of them already have, and the others are probably planning to do so in order to get tenure at their universities). Yes, the people of the time didn't think that the deposition of Romulus was any big deal, or that the empire had fallen, but I can't help it if they weren't paying attention. Yes, there was still another surviving claimant to the throne, a former emperor who'd been kicked out of Italy by Romulus' father and was now hanging out in Illyria insisting that he was still emperor of the west. However, nobody took him seriously, and he died in Illyria in 480. And yes, there was still a so-called "Roman" emperor in Constantinople, not just in 476, but for almost a thousand years after that. But using the term "Roman Empire" for a Constantinople-based, mostly Greek-speaking eastern Mediterranean state that didn't even own the city of Rome just seems silly to me, even if the easterners called themselves Romans all the way up till 1453. Even when an eastern emperor named Justinian reconquered Italy for a while in the 6th century, he didn't move back to Rome or even Ravenna; Italy under Justinian was just a dependency of an eastern empire that would come to be known to modern historians as Byzantine (from Byzantium, the former name of Constantinople).

Romulus Augustulus was the last Roman emperor who lived in Italy, and for whom Italy, with its Latin-speaking population, its senators in the city of Rome, and its ancient traditions, was the center of the empire. When he fell, and Italy became a barbarian kingdom, the Roman Empire fell. Ba-da-bing, ba-da-boom. Or, if you don't like that line of reasoning, we can always fall back on the tremendous symbolism of the name Romulus and the nickname Augustulus. The city of Rome was founded by Romulus, and the empire was founded by Augustus. What could be more fitting than that the last Roman emperor should be named Romulus Augustulus?

Nothing, that's what. And so our story has come to an end. Except that maybe we should have an epilogue to tell you what happened after Rome fell.

The Last Emperors

Just in case you want to know, here are the names and a few key facts about the western emperors from Valentinian III onward. They're mostly not very exciting, but it seemed a shame to leave them out. You'll note a few years when there was no emperor, usually because Ricimer was having trouble deciding on a nominee.

Petronius Maximus (455)—Roman senator, urged Valentinian III to kill Aetius, named himself emperor after Valentinian's death. Killed by a mob in Rome when he proved unable to protect the city from the Vandals.

Avitus (455-456)—Supporter of Petronius Maximus, named emperor by the Visigoths and Gallo-Romans after Petronius' death. Deposed and later killed by Ricimer and Majorian.

Majorian (457-461)—Competent general and colleague of Ricimer, who killed him when it looked like Majorian might be getting too independent-minded.

Libius Severus (461-465)—Nonentity installed by Ricimer, whose puppet he remained. Probably died a natural death, although it was later claimed that Ricimer poisoned him.

Anthemius (467-472)—Greek-speaking eastern general, nominated by the eastern empire, accepted by Ricimer to seal an anti-Vandal alliance. Had a falling out with Ricimer, who overthrew and killed him.

Olybrius (472)—Roman senator, married to Valentinian III's daughter, installed as emperor by Ricimer. Died shortly after Ricimer himself died in 472.

Glycerius (473-474)—Roman general installed by Ricimer's nephew Gundobad, king of the Burgundians. Deposed by Julius Nepos under the authority of the eastern empire, he ended up becoming a bishop.

Julius Nepos (474-475)—Roman general in Illyria, commissioned by eastern empire to overthrow and replace Glycerius, which he did with little difficulty. Overthrown himself by a general named Orestes, Julius fled back to Illyria and claimed to be western emperor until his death in 480.

Romulus Augustulus (475-476)—Son of Orestes, installed as emperor by his father, deposed by Odoacer. Sent to live on an estate in southern Italy, ultimate fate unrecorded. No doubt he died eventually.

Epilogue: The Post-Roman World

While the western empire was collapsing, the eastern empire had trundled merrily along, especially after the Huns stopped ravaging the Balkans. Emperor succeeded emperor, normally without too much bloodshed, and the civil authorities in Constantinople managed to avoid losing all power to the military. However, there was a small problem involving unruly Ostrogoths, some of whom, once Attila's empire had fallen apart, had wandered into the Balkans and appropriated land for themselves. To get rid of them, in the late 5th century a clever eastern Emperor named Zeno told them they could go take over Italy with his blessing, provided they overthrew that upstart Odoacer first. The Ostrogoths took him up on the offer, and set up a very successful kingdom in Italy under their king Theodoric.

Eastern Emperors from Arcadius to Justinian	
Arcadius	395-408
Theodosius II	408-450
Marcian	450-457
Leo I	457-474
Leo II	474
Zeno	474-491
Anastasius	491-518
Justin I	518-527
Justinian I	527-565

Farther west, the Visigoths conquered most of Spain, though the Suevi kept their bit in the northwest. As for Gaul, the Visigoths grabbed the entire southwest, the Burgundians expanded in the southeast, and the Franks took most of the north (knocking off the Alamanni along the way). In the 6th century, the Franks would go on to whup up on both the Visigoths and the Burgundians, and eventually would become the rulers of almost all of Gaul. The far northwest, however, got taken over by refugees from Britain, whose descendants are called Bretons to this day. The refugees were fleeing Britain because it was being invaded from the east by Saxons and the closely related Angles, both of them north German tribes. The British, who, as you remember, had been cut loose by the empire back in Honorius' day, had originally hired the Anglo-Saxons as mercenaries to help them fight off attacks from the Scots and Picts. Surprise, surprise, the mercenaries didn't go home when their contract ran out: instead, they spent the next few centuries slowly conquering most of Britain.

The Vandals were happy with their kingdom in Africa, and Mauretania, like the non-Anglo-Saxon parts of Britain, had slipped into the control of indigenous chieftains. Thus, by the year 500, there was no Roman turf left in the west, as shown on the map below. As previously mentioned, an emperor named Justinian tried to revive the Roman Empire in the 6th century by conquering Africa, Italy, and part of Spain. The conquest was successful, but it didn't Romanize the empire, and much of Italy was lost to the Lombards (yet another Germanic tribe) soon after Justinian's death. Then in the 7th century, Arabs, inspired by their new religion of Islam, conquered all of the Middle East except for Asia Minor, as well as all of north Africa. At the same time, Slavs took over most of the Balkans. Justinian's attempt to re-establish the Roman Empire had failed, meaning our story really is finished now. Except for the consolatory postlude.

Extensive Questions for Chapter Ten

1. When did the Roman Empire fall?
   - (a) 324, when Constantine I defeated Licinius and became sole emperor
   - (b) 330, when Constantine I announced that Constantinople was open for business
   - (c) 337, when Constantine I died
   - (d) 363, when Julian, the last pagan emperor, was killed
   - (e) 395, when Theodosius I, last sole ruler of the united empire, died
   - (f) 410, when the Visigoths sacked Rome
   - (g) 454, when Aetius was killed
   - (h) 455, when Valentinian III was killed
   - (i) 476, when Romulus Augustulus was deposed
   - (j) 480, when Julius Nepos died in Illyria
   - (k) 565, when Justinian died
   - (l) the late 6th century, when the Lombards conquered most of Italy
   - (m) the 7th century, when the Arabs conquered the Middle East and north Africa
   - (n) 1453, when the Turks captured Constantinople
   - (o) 1806, when the Holy Roman Empire was officially dissolved[1]
   - (p) 1917, when the last Russian Czar was overthrown[2]

     Notes: [1]The so-called Holy Roman Empire was invented by medieval Germans who conquered north and central Italy and got themselves crowned western emperor by the Pope. It was essentially a Kingdom of Germany with at best weak control over parts of Italy.
     [2]The Russian Czars, having become Greek-style Christians during the Middle Ages, regarded themselves as the heirs of the Byzantine Empire after its fall, and claimed that Moscow was the Third Rome (the first two being Rome proper, and then Constantinople).

2. Why did the Roman Empire fall?
   - (a) barbarian invasions
   - (b) incompetent emperors
   - (c) corrupt bureaucracy
   - (d) unpatriotic citizens
   - (e) economic mismanagement
   - (f) decline in population
   - (g) bad luck
   - (h) some or all of the above

3. How did the Roman Empire fall?
   - (a) lengthily and confusingly, like a sentence from one of William Faulkner's books
   - (b) violently yet tediously, like Peter Jackson's version of *King Kong*
   - (c) angrily and disjointedly, like a drunk arguing with the guy on the next bar stool over
   - (d) sadly yet resignedly, like Henry Clay when he realized he'd never be President
   - (e) softly and suddenly, like someone who's met up with a Snark of the Boojum variety
   - (f) some or all of the above

4. Of the people featured in this chapter, which three are the most famous today? *Hint: One had a city in the eastern empire named after him, but now it's changed its name to Istanbul; another has a city in Florida named after him; the third, perhaps the most famous of all even though he wasn't even a Roman, often gets his name misspelled, with two l's instead of one.*

(a) Emperor Petronius Maximus
(b) Ricimer
(c) St. Augustine
(d) Emperor Miami VIII
(e) Attila the Hun

(f) St. Daytona of the Beach
(g) Genghis Khan
(h) Emperor Constantine I
(i) Arbogast the Frank
(j) Stephen Báthory the Hungarian

5. What modern-day country do you suppose takes its name from the Franks, who conquered almost all of Gaul in the early Middle Ages and then renamed it after themselves?
    (a) France   (b) Italy   (c) Japan

6. What modern-day country do you suppose takes its name from the Angles, who, together with the Saxons, invaded Britain in the 5th and 6th centuries and eventually conquered most of the island?
    (a) England   (b) Germany   (c) Burkina Faso

7. What modern-day German state do you suppose derives its name from those Saxons who, instead of going off to invade Britain like other Saxons did, stayed at home in northwest Germany?
    (a) Lower Saxony   (b) Brandenburg   (c) North Rhine-Westphalia

8. What kind of wine do you think comes from the region of France where the Burgundians settled?
    (a) burgundy   (b) champagne   (c) pinot grigio

9. The name of which ancient tribe is the source of the modern words meaning "Germany" in Spanish and French (the words are *Alemania* and *Allemagne*, respectively)?
    (a) Alamanni   (b) Californi   (c) Etruscans

10. How many chapters of a Roman history book should be devoted to the late empire?
    (a) zero   (b) one   (c) ten or twenty

Answers: 1. (i)
                    2. (h)
                    3. (f)
                    4. (c), (e), and (h)
                    5. (a)
                    6. (a)
                    7. (a)
                    8. (a)
                    9. (a)
                    10. (b)

Consolatory Postlude

Thursday night, circa 2000 AD, in a dorm study lounge, where a few students are discussing the history of Rome in preparation for a test on Friday. (Why they're actually talking about the course material, instead of about things like movies or the meaning of life, is unclear to me. It seems a bit unusual for a pre-test study session.)

STUDENT A: I feel bad for the Romans. They spent all that time building up their empire, and then it got carved up by a bunch of barbarians.

STUDENT B: Hey, it's not so bad. I mean, look where they started out, a few semi-civilized Latin speakers who decided to build a city. Who would've guessed they'd end up creating one of history's greatest empires?

STUDENT C: *(who's just come back into the room with a newly-opened wine cooler in her hand)* That's right. Besides, Rome itself was still a major city even after the empire collapsed. And it's definitely a major city today. I know, I've been there.

STUDENT A: Oh, you've been there? What's it like?

STUDENT C: Yeah, I went there for about a week the summer before my junior year. You know, it's got ruins, nightclubs, art, architecture. And a lot of motor scooters.

STUDENT B: Did you go to the Forum?

STUDENT C: Yeah, and I climbed up the Palatine Hill. Oh, and there's a lot of churches too. And the churches are full of art.

The City of Rome
in the Late 5th Century AD

STUDENT D: *(not very interested)* Uh-huh. So, are we gonna order pizza or what?

STUDENT A: *(who was raised Catholic, but isn't particularly devout)* Oh, that's right! The Pope lives in Rome, doesn't he?

STUDENT E: *(who took a medieval history course last year)* I've got some Domino's coupons in my room. Yeah, the popes kept living there after the emperors left, so Rome didn't disappear even in the Middle Ages. But it shrunk a lot.

STUDENT C: I vote for veggie lover's.

STUDENT A: Okay, so the city survived, but the empire fell apart. And the Germans took over everything.

STUDENT B: Sort of, but they ended up getting absorbed into post-Roman civilization. I mean, like French, Italian, Spanish, they're all Romance languages. Basically Latin, only different, because languages change over time.

STUDENT D: *(who took a course in the History of English last term)* Dude, you're like way too into this. Besides, English isn't a Romance language.

STUDENT C: *(to Student A)* Did you mean "Okay, let's get veggie lovers," or "Okay, the city's still around"?

STUDENT E: *(who also took the course in History of English, but paid more attention than Student D)* Could we get something with meat on it? And by the way, even English is full of words borrowed from Latin.

STUDENT A: Like what?

STUDENT E: I dunno, August? Cheese? Superintendent?

STUDENT D: *(getting interested despite himself)* Yeah, and don't, like, a lot of modern legal systems go back to the Romans too?

STUDENT C: Ugh, could we please not talk about law? Next thing you know, Dave's gonna start talking about accounting.

STUDENT E: Well, excuse me, Miss English Literature Major. At least I'm gonna have a job when I graduate. And besides, accounting is cool once you get into it.

STUDENT B: Oh, for God's sake. For the last time, accounting is not cool.

STUDENT C: Well, neither is law. You're just planning on going to law school because you want to make a lot of money.

STUDENT B: What's wrong with making a lot of money?

STUDENT A: Could we get back to the Romans? I wanna know what you think the essay questions are gonna be about.

STUDENT C: Well, I bet one of them is going to be about what we've just been talking about, you know, the enduring influence of Roman civilization, etc. I mean, don't you remember all that stuff about how, like, even stuff like the calendar comes from the Romans, and now the whole world uses it? You know, like August, and everything. And leap years?

STUDENT B: I don't remember that. I must've missed class that day.

STUDENT D: Yeah, but it was in the book, man. I thought you always read the book.

STUDENT C: Anyway, the point is, Rome had a tremendous influence on western civilization. Art, literature, language, government, whatever. Just throw out a few examples and you'll do great on the essay.

STUDENT B: Can I take a look at your notes?

STUDENT A: Me too.

STUDENT E: I've got it in my notes too. But look, can we get back to pizza first?

STUDENT A: Good idea. I'm hungry.

STUDENT D: I want pepperoni on mine.

STUDENT C: Okay, look, there are five of us, we're gonna need two larges anyway. Let's get one veggie lover's, and one with pepperoni and...

STUDENT B: Mushrooms?

STUDENT E: Fine with me.

STUDENT A: Okay.

STUDENT D: *(pulling out his cell phone)* Okay, I'll order if you go get your coupons. *(Student E gets up and goes out into the hallway)*. Hey, did you eat any pizza when you were in Rome?

STUDENT C: Yeah, it's not bad. But I liked the Forum better.

STUDENT A: Sounds nice. I'd like to go there sometime. I guess the Romans did all right for themselves after all.

STUDENT B: Yeah, a lot better than the Etruscans, Parthians, or Visigoths. You don't see any of those guys around anymore.

STUDENT E: *(re-entering the room with a sheet of pizza coupons in his hand)* Bad news, guys. I don't have any coupons for two larges.

STUDENT B: Oh, for the love of...All right, what do you have coupons for?

And the discussion carries on from there. I'm afraid it might be quite a while before they get any pizza.

Index of Personal Names

Aemilian, forgettable emperor, 91

Aemilius Paullus, Lucius, Roman general, 17, 18, 22

Aetius, western generalissimo during the reign of Valentinian III, 118-120, 121, 123

Agrippa, Marcus Vipsanius, friend of Augustus and, as luck would have it, an excellent general, 52, 53, 55, 58

Agrippina, wife of Claudius and mother of Nero, 65-66

Alaric, Visigothic leader, 117-118

Alexander Severus, Mamma's-boy emperor, 89, 90

Alexander the Great, Macedonian king whose conquest of Persia inspired several Romans to attempt similar feats, generally with unfortunate results, 53, 54, 86, 87-88, 114

Ammianus Marcellinus, Roman historian, 112

Anastasius, competent eastern emperor, 122

Ancus Marcius, boring king, 3-4, 11

Anthemius, western emperor of eastern origin, 121

Anthony, Marc, pop singer, 45

Antinous, Hadrian's "special friend", 75, 77

Antiochus the Great, king who turned out not to be so great after all, 16, 17, 18

Antoninus Pius, kind and gentle emperor, 78, 98-99

Antonius, Lucius, brother of Mark Antony, 52

Antony, Mark (Latin name **Marcus Antonius**), Roman general and manly man, 44-45, 49, 52-54, 57, 104

Aper, supposed murderer of Numerian, 101

Aphrodite, Greek goddess of love, 31

Appian, Greek writer on Roman history, 80

Apuleius, Lucius, Roman novelist, 80

Arbogast, Frankish general in Roman service, 116, 124

Arcadius, wimpy eastern emperor, 116, 118, 122

Arminius, Germanic chieftain, 55

Astaire, Fred, American dancer, star of stage and screen, 56

Atia, Caesar's niece and mother of Augustus, 41

Attalus III, king of Pergamum, 19

Attila the Hun, nicknamed "The Scourge of God", short, horse-riding barbarian leader who, according to one report, died of a nosebleed, 118, 119, 120, 121, 124

Augustine, St., author of *The Confessions* and *The City of God*, 112-113, 124

Augustus (original name **Gaius Octavius**, known to us as **Octavian** 44-27 BC and **Augustus** thereafter), lousy general, unremarkable orator, and outstanding emperor, 35, 41, 44-45, 47, 49, 52-59, 63, 65, 80, 87, 98-99, 104, 121, 125

Aurelian, optimistic emperor, 92, 98-100, 105, 125

Avidius Cassius, Gaius, Roman general, 78-79

Avitus, short-term western emperor, 121

Balbinus, feeble co-emperor, 90, 93

Balbus, Marcus Atius, Caesar's brother-in-law, 33

Bibulus, Marcus Calpurnius, ineffective Optimate, 39

Bogus (a.k.a. **Bogud**), king of Mauretania, 35

Bonaparte, Napoleon, Emperor of the French and famous short guy, 1, 15, 18, 23, 97, 105

Boswell, James, Scottish biographer, 83

Brutus, Lucius Junius, founder of the Roman Republic, 4, 45

Brutus, Marcus Junius, assassin, 44-46

Caesar, Gaius Julius, Roman general, dictator, and balding bon vivant, *ii*, *ix*, 33-34, 35, 37, 38-47, 48, 49, 52, 54, 56, 58, 66, 70, 80,112

Caligula, depraved and incompetent emperor, 64, 65, 70, 72, 113

Camillus, Marcus, furious patrician, 5-6

Capone, Al, American criminal, 38

Caracalla, tyrannical tough-guy emperor, 87-88, 125

Carinus, unexciting emperor, 100-101

Carter, Jimmy, American president, 90

Carus, emperor who wanted to found a dynasty, 100-101

Cassius Longinus, Gaius, assassin, 44-46

Catiline (Latin name **Lucius Sergius Catilina**), dissolute patrician rabble-rouser and revolutionary, 37, 38, 42, 58

Cato, Marcus Porcius, "the Censor", grumpy Roman senator, 13, 17, 18, 22, 24, 28, 31, 42, 58

Cato, Marcus Porcius, "the Younger", die-hard foe of Caesar, 42, 43

Catullus, Gaius Valerius, Roman lyric poet, 58

Charles, Prince of Wales, 72

Churchill, Winston, British prime minister, 1

Cicero, Marcus Tullius, Roman orator and politician, *ix*, 37, 38-46, 47, 58

Cinna, Lucius Cornelius, anti-Sulla consul, 29-30, 33, 42

Claudius, pedantic emperor, 65, 72, 98, 99

Claudius Gothicus, Goth-killing emperor, 92, 98-99, 100

Claudius, Appius, consul, roadbuilder, and intransigent senior senator, 6

Clay, Henry, American senator, 123

Cleopatra, queen of Egypt, 35, 43, 45, 52-54, 59, 71

Clodius, Publius, violent demagogic politician, 40-42

Commodus, nutty emperor, 46, 79, 86, 87, 93

Constans, son of Constantine, unexciting western emperor, 113-114

Constantine the Great, Christianizing emperor, 103-104, 105, 107, 110-113, 123, 124, 125

Constantine II, emperor whose lack of fraternal feeling got him in trouble, 113

Constantius, tetrarchal emperor and father of Constantine the Great, 101-103, 104, 105

Constantius II, beleaguered eastern emperor, 113-114

Corleone, Vito, fictional crime boss, 1

Cornelia, Cinna's daughter and first wife of Caesar, 33, 40

Crassus, Marcus Licinius, wealthy Roman politician who learned that fighting slaves was easier than fighting Parthians, 30, 31, 34, 35, 36, 37, 38-42, 47, 52, 53

Cybele, Asiatic mother goddess, 71

Decius, emperor killed by Goths, 91

Didius Julianus, emperor who bought the throne, 86, 93

Diocletian, successful despotic emperor whose convoluted plan for the succession didn't work out, 99, 101-103, 104, 110, 111, 125

Domitian, domineering emperor, 70, 72, 76, 79, 80, 81, 125

Drusus, Marcus Livius, tribune, 29, 30

Drusus, Tiberius' brother, 55

Elagabalus, outlandish emperor, 88-89, 90, 93, 113

Elizabeth II, queen of England, 93, 105

Eugenius, puppet emperor, 116

Eumenes II, king of Pergamum, 17, 19

Fabius Maximus, Quintus, Roman general, 23

Faulkner, William, American author, 123

Florian, inconsequential emperor, 100

Foreman, George, heavyweight champion, 10

Freud, Sigmund, Austrian psychoanalyst, 66

Frost, Robert, American poet, author of "The Gift Outright", 73

Fulvia, wife of Antony, 57-58

Gabinius, Aulus, pro-Pompey tribune, 37

Gaiseric, Vandal king, 119

Galba, stingy old emperor, 68, 72

Galerius, Christian-hating tetrarchal emperor, 101-104, 105

Galla Placidia, sister of Arcadius and Honorius, 118

Gallienus, emperor who did what he could under trying circumstances, 91, 92, 98, 105

Gallus, Trebonianus, Goth-fearing emperor, 91

Gellius, Aulus, Roman essayist, 80

Genghis Khan, medieval Mongol conqueror, 124

Geta, short-lived co-emperor, 87

Gibbon, Edward, British author of *The History of the Decline and Fall of the Roman Empire*, 79, 83, 110

Glabrio, Manius Acilius, unmilitary consul, 37

Glycerius, western emperor who became a bishop, 121

Gordian I, not much of an emperor, 90

Gordian II, not much of an emperor, 90

Gordian III, only slightly more of an emperor than his grandfather and father, 90-91

Gracchus, Gaius Sempronius, tribune, 20-21, 22, 23, 25

Gracchus, Tiberius Sempronius, tribune, 19-20, 22, 23, 25

Gratian, western emperor, 115-116

Hadrian, Greek-loving emperor, 75, 77-78, 80, 81, 125

Hamilcar Barca, Carthaginian general, 7-8, 10

Hannibal, Carthaginian general who bit off more than he could chew, 8-10, 11, 16, 86, 87, 115

Hasdrubal, brother of Hannibal, 8, 9, 10

Hasdrubal, brother-in-law of Hannibal, 10

Hasdrubal, opponent of Scipio Aemilianus, 11, 18

Hasdrubal, son of Gisco, 9, 10

Hayes, Alfred, American writer, author of "Joe Hill", 25

Helena, St., mother of Constantine, 97, 105

Hercules, mythological tough guy, 86, 93

Herod the Great, king of Judea, 53

Homer, Greek epic poet, 31

Honorius, do-nothing western emperor, 113, 116-118, 122

Horace (Latin name **Quintus Horatius Flaccus**), Roman lyric poet, 58

128

Humpty-Dumpty, egg, *v*, 97

Isis, Egyptian goddess, 71, 80

Jackson, Peter, New Zealand filmmaker, 123

Jerome, St., Bible translator, 112

Jesus Christ, suspected troublemaker, 56, 64, 66, 71, 105

Jones, Indiana, cinematic action hero, 76

Jovian, stopgap emperor, 114

Jugurtha, king of Numidia, 28, 58

Julia, Caesar's aunt and wife of Marius, 33

Julia, Caesar's sister and wife of M. Atius Balbus, 33, 41, 45

Julia, Caesar's daughter and wife of Pompey, 40-42, 45

Julia, Augustus' only child, and, frankly, a big disappointment to him, 57

Julia Domna, wife of Septimius Severus, 87, 88

Julia Maesa, Julia Domna's sister and grandmother of Elagabalus and Alexander Severus, 88-89

Julia Mamaea, mother of Alexander Severus, 88-89

Julia Soaemias, mother of Elagabalus, 88-89

Julian, shockingly pagan emperor, 114, 115, 123

Julius Nepos, penultimate western emperor, 121, 123

Jupiter, paternal sky god, 4, 13, 37, 99, 101, 103

Justin, illiterate eastern emperor, 122

Justinian, eastern emperor who tried to reconquer the west, 121, 122, 123

Juvenal (Latin name **Decimus Junius Juvenalis**), Roman satirist, 80

Kardashian, Kim, pop-culture phenom, 93

Kim Il-Sung, North Korean dictator, 56-57

Lancelot, Sir, knight of the Round Table, 20

Leo I, long-lived eastern emperor, 122

Leo II, short-lived eastern emperor, 122

Lepidus, Marcus Aemilius, consul and unsuccessful revolutionary, 31, 34, 36, 42, 49

Lepidus, Marcus Aemilius, triumvir, 45, 49, 52, 57

Libius Severus, puppet western emperor, 121

Licinius, post-tetrarchal emperor, 103-104, 107, 123

Livia, wife of Augustus and mother of Tiberius, 56, 57

Livius Andronicus, Lucius, early Latin poet, 31

Livy (Latin name **Titus Livius**), Roman historian, 3-4, 58, 91

Lucan (Latin name **Marcus Annaeus Lucanus**), Roman epic poet, 75, 80

Lucius Verus, mediocre co-emperor, 78

Lucullus, Lucius Licinius, Roman general who fought against Mithridates, 37

Macrinus, praetorian prefect who became emperor, 88

Magnus Maxiumus, usurper, 116

Mago, Carthaginian general, 10

Mahan, Alfred, author of a book called *The Influence of Sea Power upon History*, 7

Majorian, last competent western emperor, 121

Marcian, vigorous eastern emperor, 121, 122

Marcus Aurelius, philosopher-emperor who shouldn't have had a son, 78-79, 80, 81, 86, 87

Marius, Gaius, Roman general, 28-29, 30, 32, 33, 42, 46, 47

Mars, god of war, 4, 89

Martial (Latin name **Marcus Valerius Martialis**), Roman humorist, 75, 80

Marx, Karl, political and economic theorist, 65

Mary, mother of Jesus, 54

Maxentius, son of Maximian who made himself emperor, 103-104, 105

Maximian, co-emperor with Diocletian, 101-103, 104, 105

Maximinus Daia, anti-Christian tetrarchal emperor, 103-104, 105

Maximinus Thrax (the latter word is Latin for "Thracian"), soldier emperor, 90, 93, 105

Maximus Decimus Meridius, fictional general in the movie *Gladiator*, 46

Medusa, mythical monster whose horrific visage petrified those who gazed upon it, 17

Michelangelo, Renaissance artist, 81

Milo, Titus Annius, tribune, opponent of Clodius, 41-42

Mithras, Persian warrior god, 71

Mithridates, king of Pontus, 28-30, 33, 34, 37, 38, 39

Nero, cruel and scandalous emperor, 63, 65-66, 68, 69, 70, 72, 80, 87, 125

Nerva, elderly emperor, 76

Numa Pompilius, pious king, 3, 4

Numerian, short-term co-emperor, 100-101

Octavia, Augustus' sister and wife of Antony, 53-54

Octavian, see *Augustus*

Octavius, Gaius, see *Augustus*

Octavius, Gnaeus, anti-Cinna consul, 29

Odoacer, German general who deposed Romulus Augustulus, 120, 121, 122

Oedipus, mythological Theban king who loved his mother, 46

Olybrius, short-lived western emperor, 121

Orestes, father of Romulus Augustulus, 121

Otho, short-lived emperor, 68-69, 72, 76

Ovid (Latin name **Publius Ovidius Naso**), Roman poet, 58

Paine, Thomas, British-American essayist, 83

Perseus, king of Macedonia, 17

Pertinax, short-term emperor, 86

Petronius (first name uncertain), Roman novelist, 80

Petronius Maximus, senator who made himself emperor, 120, 121, 124

Phaedrus, handsome young Athenian, 77

Philip the Arab, run-of-the-mill emperor, 91

Philip V, king of Macedonia, 13, 16, 17

Picard, Jean-Luc, Starfleet officer, 54

Plato, Greek philosopher, 17

Plautus, Titus Maccius, comic playwright, 31

Pliny the Elder (Latin name **Gaius Plinius Secundus**), Roman science writer, 80

Pliny the Younger (Latin name **Gaius Plinius Caecilius Secundus**), Roman letter-writer, 80

Plutarch, Greek biographer and essayist, 80

Polybius, Greek author of a history of Rome and the Mediterranean, 17, 18

Pompeius Strabo, Gnaeus, Roman general, father of Pompey the Great, 29, 30

Pompeius, Gnaeus, "Pompey the Great", Roman general who shouldn't have fled to Egypt, 30, 31, 33, 34, 35, 36-43, 45, 47, 52, 54, 80, 125

Pompeius, Sextus, son of Pompey the Great, 52-53, 54

Popeye, sailor man, 45

Postumus, Marcus Cassianus Latinius, Gallic emperor, 85, 91, 92

Probus, not a bad emperor, under the circumstances, 100

Prusias, king of Bithynia, 17

Ptolemy Apion, king of Cyrene, 29

Pupienus, feeble co-emperor, 90, 93

Pyrrhus, semi-Greek king, 6, 7, 9

Quintilian (Latin name **Marcus Fabius Quintilianus**), Roman rhetorician, 80

Quirinus, obscure god, 3, 4, 33

Quintillus, nonentity emperor, 92, 98

Reagan, Ronald, American president, 7

Remus, twin who would have been better off if he'd been an only child, 3

Ricimer, general and emperor-maker in the west, 120, 121, 124

Romulus, legendary founder and first king of Rome, 3, 4, 9, 33, 121

Romulus Augustulus, last Roman emperor, 120-121, 123

Sallust (Latin name **Gaius Sallustius Crispus**), Roman historian, 58

Saturninus, Lucius Appuleius, tribune, 28

Scipio, Lucius Cornelius, younger brother of Africanus Major, 16, 17, 22

Scipio, Publius Cornelius, "Africanus Major", Roman general, 9-10, 13, 16, 17, 22

Scipio Aemilianus, Publius Cornelius, "Africanus Minor", Roman general, 10, 18, 19, 20, 22, 23

Scipio Nasica, Publius Cornelius, who thought Carthage should be preserved, 18, 22

Sejanus, Lucius Aelius, praetorian prefect, 64

Seneca, Lucius Annaeus, playwright, philosopher, and imperial counselor, 65-66, 75, 80

Septimius Severus, pretty successful emperor, 86-87, 88, 125

Sertorius, Quintus, die-hard anti-Sullan who holed up in Spain for several years, 30, 31, 34, 36

Servius Tullius, king who didn't build a wall, 4, 63

Severus, tetrarchal emperor about whom little is known, 103

Socrates, Greek philosopher, 77

Spartacus, leader of a slave revolt, 34, 36

Stalin, Joseph, Soviet dictator and all-around bad guy, 8

Stephen Báthory, Hungarian prince who became king of Poland, 124

Stilicho, western generalissimo during the reign of Honorius, 116-117

Suetonius Tranquillus, Gaius, Roman biographer, 80

Sulla, Lucius Cornelius, Roman general and dictator, 28-31, 32, 33-34, 36, 37, 39, 42, 45, 46, 47, 54

Sulpicius Rufus, Publius, tribune, 29

Tacitus, emperor who had the same name as a famous historian, 100

Tacitus, Publius Cornelius (actually, his first name might be **Gaius**—there's conflicting evidence), Roman historian, 80, 112

Tarquinius Priscus, immigrant king, 4, 45

Tarquinius Superbus, arrogant king, 4, 45

Terence (Latin name **Publius Terentius Afer**), comic playwright, 31

Terwilliger, Robert, "Sideshow Bob", fictional TV villain, 9

Theodoric, king of the Ostrogoths, 122

Theodosius, last emperor to rule both east and west, 113, 115-117, 123

Theodosius II, eastern emperor, 118, 119, 122

Thurber, James, American author, 17

Tiberius, gloomy-minded emperor, 55, 56, 64, 65, 66, 72

Titus, popular emperor, *iv*, 69, 70, 72, 78, 125

Trajan, conquering emperor, 75, 76-77, 80, 81, 87, 98-99, 114, 125

Trump, Donald, rich guy who became US president, 93

Tullus Hostilius, warlike king, 3

Tyson, Mike, professional boxer, 93

Valens, emperor who should've been more careful at Adrianople, 114, 115

Valentinian, emperor who went west, 114-115

Valentinian II, child emperor, 115, 116

Valentinian III, western emperor who wasn't up to the job, 118, 120, 121, 123

Valerian, captive emperor, 85, 91, 100, 101

Vercingetorix, Gaul whose utter failure as a rebel somehow qualifies him for French national hero status, 42

Verres, Gaius, corrupt governor, 37

Vergil (Latin name **Publius Vergilius Maro**), Roman epic poet, 58, 112

Verginius Rufus, Lucius, general who refused to be made emperor, 76

Vespasian, down-to-earth emperor, 69-70, 72

Vitellius, gluttonous emperor, 68-69, 72

Wood, Grant, American painter, 95

YHWH, god of Israel, 71

Zeno, clever eastern emperor, 121, 122

Zenobia, Palmyrene queen, 85, 92

A Present-Day View of the Roman Forum
As Seen from the Capitoline Hill

CPSIA information can be obtained
at www.ICGtesting.com
Printed in the USA
BVHW01s1917130818
524388BV00008B/183/P